CONFLUENCE

POEMS BY RON ANDROLA
(2015)

Busted Dharma Books

Book design by Kurt Nimmo

Author photograph © 2015 by Ann Androla
Cover photograph © 2015 by Kurt Nimmo

Some of these poems have appeared online & in print (some in altered
form) at Big Hammer, Gypsy Art Show, Lost & Found Times, Busted
Dharma, Red Fez, Zygote in My Coffee, Goss 183, MIPOesias. Thanks
to all involved. An acknowledging thank you to Jim Valvis, Didi
Menendez, Kurt Nimmo, Cee Williams, & Chuck Joy.

First Printing: 2015

ISBN-13: 978-0692554128

Busted Dharma Books
404 Hudgins Street
Smithville, Texas 78957

www.busteddharma.com/books

FOR ANN

A special thanks to Ann Androla

for careful editing
for love
years
& luck

INTRODUCTION

We are made of stars. Our thoughts are made of stars & cosmic dust. Our glands, dreams, intentions, passions, idiotic philosophies, memories, & our dramas are made of stars & cosmic molecules; hence our poems. Languages, hesitations, cultural conundrums, crickets increasing tinnitus & depression, the pyramids, histories, lust, are all made by stars & cosmic fluctuations. Any human invention, any last green giraffe, any whisper from the beds of the dead, is made of stars & cosmic energy. Murder, police brutality, pop songs, political stances, the hollow moon, grown from stars & cosmic guts. Clocks, clouds, blood; logic, magic, minutes, 57 alien races, are creations of stars & cosmic fabric. We are everything. Everything is poetry.

This book has flowed into existence from various points of perspective & time. I hope the poems swirl into a colorful surprise for you. Smiling is optional.

Ron Androla, summer 2015

The Yes of No

A man wakes on a dark morning.
He's been dreaming about feathers
cascading from his ears, falling
down his arms. He wonders if a
golden bird has exploded inside
his head. By the time water splashes
onto his face the dream
vaporizes, but for soft, far,
imaginary
fluff.

Lighting My Nose

Burning my brain. Smoke
twirls like thin, escaping,
headless dancers out & up
the sides of my head. I spin
I see. I listen
I taste
feelings from very old days.
I smell dead cigars & garlic
in New Castle, Pennsylvania,
circa 1960, when everything
was something else & quite
Syrian. This bulbous, aging
atomic bomb in the center of my face.
An existential fuse, nose-hairs
lit. Plus 40 years whiskey
fat. Uncle Al, yr
genes pepper over
the fires of life with
iron ore dust. Now I look
like you as an old man.
Veins in my eyes burst
& water. They appear
painful, yr eyes, my
eyes, full of backdrop smoke.

No Shit

I'm suddenly very conscious & I'm
already getting out of our bed. It's
6 in the morning & I know it's my
turn for the dog, Ann established that
last night. Yeah, first I put myself
together, treat the cats, call our old
dog downstairs to go outside.
He walks, head-bent, slow click
Astaire over linoleum. I stumble
feel in the dark garage. Slippers.
A poem woke me. First there was a
line that didn't wake me, but the
next line whispered its echo from
my toothless lips as I scrambled
out of black sheets. Of course,
of course, the words weren't
retained, which is fine, really,
it happens. There are so many
preambles crusting an eventual
poem. Don't be alarmed,
you're inside a poem.

Concentration between Coffee

Mahogany bean salad. I am thinking
of numbers, chances, odd odds, Frank
Zappa, mango salad.

Everything depends
upon triangulation
strangling a chicken in 20th century rain.

As a consequence digression shits
translucent wheelbarrows of
clover honey over every coin I

rub, say, thumb
skin becomes
palatable dished on a yellow leaf.

I've sipped all the mosquitoes,
sweetheart.
I'm hearing more than plums bleed.

I Write Poems Because

It's Tuesday. There are other things I cld & shld do, but as I age I find the urge & the need to write demands immediate attention – if I don't write it, a poem doesn't appear. When I feel my fingers typing on the keyboard & the voice somewhere behind my nose begins an articulation, I must concentrate & focus & let the rest of things I cld & shld do, go. But I can't lie to you, most times words aren't ringing my fingers & the voice somewhere behind my nose is just a puff of fog across a black pond. There are so many other things to do. I write poems because a poem is an internal relief-valve, necessary for continuing survival. I write poems because the process of forming the connecting words intensifies my own experience, & it's mental fun. Related to dopamine or something in the brain – it feels good to nail molecules to the rush of eternity. I write poems because the waves pooling behind my neck recede & I can pull my chin out of the sand, even stand up to speak at the sky. I write poems because I don't want to drown. I write poems because few read them, the most zen pure art there is to practice. I write poems because human existence triangulates word, biological creature, & the modern world.

The Elastic Pull of Neptune

Between moments floated into a black
pool my canoe flies – & the proportionate
sun slice of the day is a delicious pumpkin
pie, tho there is none, which is wonderful
& regretful, poor of pie, tho one's tongue
is the natural taste of pumpkin. Blue

vapor. Great cliffs of ice. Flight! By wing!
Ancient snow. The funky, clunky cosmos.
Take note: aliens. Real, imagined aliens.
Strutting beside a dawn power-walker,
huffing, moving with early traffic, the elastic
pull of Neptune in the mountains of Nepal.

A Bouquet

Old women & their soft flowers
in angular morning sunlight, alone,
look *right,* while old men, full of war
poison, fiddling with daisy stalks, droopy
petunias, & pink petals in a kitchen, appear
insane in a deathly proportionate
way – floral tea & dry black rock – a new
sun, the lost moon. A water mirror,
pulling a terrified fish from a loaf of bread,
a calendar burns on a wet wall.
From the touch of a perfumed finger
feathers float on sunbeam dust
canoes stemmed to pulsing dawn shore.
But men, ebbing, bones snapping,
full of gravity & foxhole prayers,
shrink, blood absorbs their skin
air, an awful loss, skeleton powder.
Old, white-haired women smile with
clam-sweet breath & smell like exploded
roses in a warm home. Dying men spit,
burping olives, exhaling sunset garlic,
undigested ganglion seeds at the sky.
Wheat pearls, partially pollinated protons,
full dentures made out of owl shit which
resemble neck wings, & words in the center
of a glass bullet, in the middle of a leafy
love
poem.
Rain, lung fog, rootless tulip
memory blooms.

Barring All Politics

You have it in yr head. I assume
yr politics are a thoughtful stance
by whatever degree necessary for
belief, or disbelief. Or maybe
you don't give a damn about
Washington & all that bullshit,
that's fine. Watching television
inside a bubble is a spiritual
event, as is weeping at dawn
& at dusk, day in, day out.
Neuronal gamma flinch.
I know you are in pain because
I see yr eyes staring at film-stars
& the split moon pulls like
taffy light from a black, final
kiss. Fast-food radiation. Pizza
pi squared like primal gristle,
pizza topped with scorched
flesh coins. All the neighbors
applaud, applaud, you are
not so different, after all, in this
cultural mud. We squeal & squeal
tiptoeing over slaughtered humans
& potato-chip bags. Let the losers &
the lost lose. From this catastrophe
art bursts our brains, fries our regrets.

Shrinking

There are places I am shrinking.
There are places I am sagging.
Parts of my body have seriously
mutated into odd flesh. Hair?
Ha. Grey as a foggy gull. My
precious ponytail strands
thin & thin. These teeth are
sculptural, ceramic, Washingtonian,
hurtful, pain of a crushed seed
injection pierce skin mountain remains.
My nipples are lit fuses.
The powder crackle chest spreads
sensitive ash worms, carbon cartoons,
mushy fucking
time. There are places I am hollow.
There are places I have thickened.
I shit red eggs. Instead of cum,
a poisonous bubble shimmers
& shivers on my blushing
head. My nipples are soft rain.
Consciousness burns the mirrors.
There's a wheatfield on my skull.
The dirt circle is pulled inward like a
pancake. Spiritual pancake
blackened & scorched by
the spin of the earth.
Sharp minutes hack melon hours.
Size? Yesterday? Stone death bones.
My voice mists with the heavy

sandalwood smoke, air in a
pumpkin room. I never feel sexy.

Digging for Inspiration

On other days I pull Ray
Carver poems thru marrow
wire, some strong Bukowski,
translated Rimbaud, W.S.
Merwin & his lice, Jack,
Beats, New York murderers,
dead Russians, dead poets,
live poets. They can energize
my funky silence so I'm
writing. At times all that's
required is a phrase, a hook,
an odd-looking look, & I begin
a poem. Maybe the poem starts
in the middle & I fill it in, or
maybe the poem is the ending
part of the poem & I go ground
up. Concentrated epiphany light
burns thru eyelids, history, & deep
earth.

Pressing Hours

A man is his art, or a
woman walks like a

slow, stoned duck. Muscle
brain full of infection,

inflections, poisonous
secretion, neuronal altitudes,

genetic luck. If you ask dead
masters to crack open shelled
poems expect enormous
silence, a nuclear walnut
when hammer meets
meat. Whispers begin
at the browned, round edge of
ground zero.

Blowing on the Incense Embers of My Fingernails

Dragon
blood, I burn cones so the furnace sucks
smoke to kiss up thru our old registers

to kiss away cat piss & cellar mold
to kiss age & ash from my face
to kiss deep & long into the odor of existence.

We paint a kitchen wall sunflower yellow,
love it, but my son comes in, laughs,
"Looks like a hippie wall now!" I don't

see the connection, but whatever, I respond,
we like the yellow. What the hell does
that have to do with hippies? I have to question.

Doug laughs. Nothin', dad, nothin',
forget what I sd. Months have passed.
I cut off most of my thin, gray ponytail.

The kitchen wall is sunflower yellow
while the whole house smells of
dragon

blood. This is not the nation
I was born in, it's an
entirely new world now.

I don't

like
it. Where's the necessary, essential poetry

of mind evolution, societal
revolution turning culture, screaming
mad fury for justice? Peace &

love are dead. Flip the coin
of light, the sun, upside
eternal tails, scorching radiation, war.

Damned, destroyed, mangled under black
televisions, sand soaked blood red, caped
in tattered, ripped flags, boys, green bricks

burst to black dust clouds
in night-vision binoculars. Turbaned
skulls begin to rain from the heavens.

They are the
bones of our
freedom. To kiss

the flesh in
the
sky, hell yes.

Poem for the Blind

He can't believe his eyes. The eye doctor's
head shoots back: "The pressure in yr eyes
is very high," he gasps like I am not
even there in a black chair, four floors up,
reading my chart on a cold Tuesday morning.

What?

The eye doctor spins & suddenly becomes
cognizant. "I'm adding other eyedrops to
the one you use now, & I want to see you
back in 2 or 3 weeks."

Oh, OK.

The eye doctor explains,
"It's a part of the aging process," &
my immediate thought in that
black chair is
fuck you, but I don't vocalize
it, just feel it pushing inside my
head, behind my eyes.

Thanksgiving, 2011

12 turkeys pirouette
over strewn crow feathers

if there was sweet eyeball
pudding in the meat of wing.

Every goddamn object is
a glass droplet of blood.

Hands shovel the trees desk
clocks & gonads, birds &

salt. Alert eye drip.
My memory is half turkey,

half semen pudding,
black moon. 12

turkeys tango with their
full-length mirrors

around a walnut table
edge warbling

to say
the clouds today are shy

pterodactyls. Coast clear.
Vinyl balloons pulse

like windy tethered
embryos over New

York City.
12 turkeys twist on 5th

Dan in a Dream

Well, you crazy son of a bitch, I
haven't even consciously thought
about you. You fucked with my
head when I first started working
at the fiberglass factory since
you were already an old-timer,
a massive black bear in sanding,
running a newer, loud machine.
Famous for fucking with those
on initial probation, 90 days.
A massive black bear
with a soft silly heart, I slowly
discover. The digital, complicated
sander for 8-foot sheets with a saw
slices yr middle finger off –
that quick, boss rushes
you to the hospital at 4
in the morning. Nobody
is trained to replace yr
antics. Months, no sander
grinds like trains over
our ancient hydraulic presses,
then you return minus a middle finger.
You think it's funny. You pretend to shoot
that finger at everyone, grinning,
bearish, indestructible.
By then, we're friends.
Last night in a dream you
smile – you win. Production

can suck yr cock, you don't
give a shit, & the company
can kiss yr big bear ass.
I always wonder if
losing that middle finger
is on purpose. A few pain
pills, bravery, closed eyes,
& the sander's circular saw.

Ann Is at Jury Duty

I do not believe we are lucky
people, but Ann intervenes
with a list of things to be
grateful, to feel lucky.
Sure there are
tubes in our nostrils,
tubes in our asses. Tubes
spinning in the marrow of
our tongue bones. Floating
like a seahorse in a bottle of
vodka a tube curls to bait a cow
hook. Morning sky squeezes, wants
to rain. Allow dim, gray clouds to
fall like a night of soaked black sheets.
Then there is always this
fish syringe, this addiction,
the tube connecting our
brain aquariums.

I Keep Quoting Glenn Close

It's all this *luggage* we carry when
we get old. She's talking to her
dead little girl. We don't know
Glenn Close's daughter is dead,

she's onscreen & sharing lunch
on a blanket in a cemetery, talking
to her mother, Glenn Close, who
sighs it's all this *luggage* we

carry when we're old. What do you
mean, mommy? The little girl questions.
Oh, nothing, nothing, forget it. Look!
I brought grapes! The girl claps triple-time.

It's all this goddamn *luggage* we
lug after many novelistic decades
pin like pulsar earrings to our face, voice,
bones, & happiness. When did happiness

fill with time's weight, & imaginary
happiness? Fattened by cultural
formulas, society bulges
with *luggage*. It is not possible

to travel light. "Travel light upon the
earth," a great poet burns into me in 1974.
I believe & live by Eigner's wisdom. But it's
all this goddamn *luggage, luggage*. Walnut

illusion shells horrible pain. Wheelchairs
gather up yolk-soaked rugs. The moon throws
hooks & quick chains across night. Glenn Close
is smiling. Her daughter has no luggage.

Join the Silence
(for Chuck Joy)

There are no silent poems. On
the French Riviera
Amerikan words evaporate
into the pull of the sun &
wide sky inhale. French
poets smoke sand &
shattered fish bones,

listen to wordless music
language, & weep.
What crybabies.
Romantic bullshit on a
misunderstood beach.
Egyptian bullshit
grunts onto the tip

of a pyramid, grinding
down & screaming at
the deaf sun. The deaf
God. Egyptian poets
accelerate their sexual
fury. They pump
pyramids full of love poems.

Join the silence in a dying
Amerikan city as poets bemoan
impending death at the beginning echo:
no hope for old men

no hope for old men
which is soundless
freedom. We just bleed.

Poetry reverses our mouths.

Tanks Fur

Tanks fur
loaded potatoes

lobbed across a murky
restaurant under

the sea. Tanks
fur breathless jelly. Tense

light bulbs burn air,
stick to my thumbs.

Tanks purr
nightmare cats;

oh they creep
upon loose snare

sensitivity. Static
electricity rubs

their vocal, visual
strings. Faulty echoes

snap voice
marrow like a crisp

pea pod. Tanks fur
the fur of the moon

the fur of the moon
light. Tanks fur

tremendous
mistakes. Pepper

spray the furious,
fur tanks. Tanks fur blood.

Wondering with a Scalpel

A lavender door
developed from
nasal evolution & high
zinc dosages injected per breath
with tarry, Russian dusk
spills crushed glass
sands, mirrors, amber chunks,
prismatic entrances.
The purple bubbles.
Their purple subatomic teeth
inside mouths made from
purple, broken windows. Purple
elephants wait ass first
curling trunks around
the lungs of old oak trees,
natural purple kites. Her
head is open, which encloses
her mind, which fills
cupboards with feathery
pillows of creamy coffee & pepper;
her scenario shrinks the sky.
Otherwise, a lavender door
stays an odd-shaped trunk
until hallucination blesses
me.

Self Portrait as a Cat

Sound fluid flood. Black bird blast.
Harpoon chipmunk amoeba
by fork tongs, penetrate
sensory, chemical reaction,
quick. Timbre of plucked
spine along the approach to
her milky lap. After
tuna & blue plasma,
dog water. Low to
earth, continuously
alert for movement,
stop a floor shadow
with two gray mica paws.

Confluence

My fingers splash on a watery keyboard.
A frog pulses inside my skull. Gathering
armfuls of lily-pads an odd poet giggles,
goads my oceanic eternity, drops those
lily-pads in my lap, roots & mud & wet
moss, too. "Syllables are the dope!" he
laughs.

We Sleep

We sleep together
while clouds, dusted
with weather, dim the moon

Stars snow up

We sleep together
& our dreams smoke
like diesel-soaked oak trunks

Above us, us

We sleep together
as decades claw
down our bones

God is firing a Venus knuckler

We sleep together
reflected &
reflecting black prisms

Milky quartz cues as souls

Blood of Thought between Us

I throw figs at a drowsy camel.
My feet are fish
swallowing, gumming
old knotty ankles like cold
vagina shoes with eyes & fluttering fins.
Fruit is always hand possible.
A bowl of olives levitates,
bursts into damaged flowers
& edge-of-city sulfur smoke.
I throw grenades at a camel carcass,
pile of meat & rug. My hands
are goddamn gulls freaking
out over mammalian slaughter at a beach.
Apples are profoundly-condensed roses.
Maple syrup: church bells where there
shldn't be church bells, mahogany-
tinted ocean sperm.

A Crow, A Caw

A crow caws over the yards.
All I hear are caws
already cawed or currently cawing.
It is just one crow, & gas-heat
rolls dust from my register,
I'm listening. Look,
the curtains are odd, pink
flamingos. Pink flower petals
stemmed to black cotton & feathery
space infinity. The crow is mold
green with tiny, fire-red eyes.
It has fangs & feeds on
humans walking down
Raspberry Street in February.
A clutter of leafy crow bites
necks on a cold, Saturday
morning. The crow no longer
caws. Our furnace rests.
Traffic pulsation. A train stitches
whispers to edges of the old doily
city. My loud ears
fill with crow echoes.

Pasta

Spaghetti sauce
breath in my
face in bed this black
morning,
I pretend you're Italian.
We live in Italy in 1960.
I crave lasagna & nicotine
as I listen to
the echoing ends
of our chickens outside
bend like windy wheat.
Pulling roots, giggling,
really, the sky is boiling.
Let
there
be
Parmesan
rain.

Some Are Saying

Some are saying we are yr children
Some are saying we are Amerikan citizens
Some are saying we are the 99%
Some are saying we are exercising our rights
Some are saying we are constitutionalists
Some are saying we are playing a rigged game
Some are saying we are now living in a police state
Some are saying we aren't focused, we're drugged
Some are saying we are dreaming dead dreams
Some are saying we are hypnotized zombies
Some are saying we are doomed to silence
Some are saying we are societal fringe dissent
Some are saying we are sodomizing billionaires
Some are saying we are disrespecting our military
Some are saying we are costing cities millions
Some are saying we are colliding with the beast
Some are saying we are forcing our views
Some are saying we are breaking laws
Some are saying we are representative of anger
Some are saying we are leftist nuts in the clouds
Some are saying we are dangerous seeds
Some are saying we are not saying anything
Some are saying we are chanting in the streets
Some are saying we are shit to the soul
Some are saying we are Amerika's last chance
Some are saying we are bothersome but avoidable
Some are saying we are innocent fools & vagrants
Some are saying we are not dancing & laughing anymore

A Sex Poem

to touch you
to feel you touch me

our vibrating
blood wires

leak & dip
& sway

tasting fast piano body
from whale-song to

the smallest bird
note as high as all

a coo is able
feathers & bone

& intrinsic wet
depth – walnut juice

a soft squirrel
jumps & hugs my face

for dear desperate life
as sperm on the black

sheets
is wet, cold, & alive

Living In History

I nail social predictions around
the edge of a silver Japanese
clock. What I see is not revolutionary
apocalypse. Blue men yank time
from the wall, positive their sanity is
necessary. "No futures see light in a prison,"
one of the officers declares with a glare.
A blue woman, a mere teen Jesus, tasers
me to the floor. Ancient carpet smells
like dog & spice bread – I amuse them.
Poets are so goddamn amusing when caught
nailing predictions around a clock.
As I recover, pouring sweat, I attempt
to sit on the floor, but I'm kicked
onto my stomach, machine-like
cuffed. Pulled to my feet. This is how
poets walk to a squad car without
poems; sore, vulnerable, miserable,
abused by the powers for
dreaming. For dreaming too loud,
in circles, stirring soup in a broken
mirror flavored by broken minutes.
Symphonic monoliths shrink like pepper
spray into the faces of a furious citizenry.
I do not mean to be true.

Heart Shaped Like a Cat's Head

I pretend you have claws.
A thin, ditsy feline
squeezes thru a gap of
bedroom door, sneezes.
Startled by the movement
of television light/shadow,
darts inside. Her name is
Bumblebee, or
Bumbles. Misogynists & dizzy
blondes of the old big screen.
Queen for a day & forever,
a gray tiara,
dead meat commercials,
tears on camera. I imagine
long, white whiskers brush
my nose as I inhale the helium
odor of sweet tuna. From yr sleeping
breath cats tumble with dust
molecules in sparking darkness. You're
all fur.

I Am Coming out as a Poet

Bravo, condemnation, or fries
with afternoon burgers on a
blue day. The reactions,
agreements, hell's fires where
brains burn because low culture
paints the flames. I am really
vulnerable & intrinsically lurid. I want
my cum leaping like phosphorescent
glandular kangaroos smelling
of sweet gasoline & Pennsylvania
farmland over my mind, my fence.
With windows down wings appear.
Lift like kite mammals. Fraternal,
feminist, violent politics, poetry, drips,
I accept the tenses of the world.
In the closet & for all my life
I was just a normal guy. Coming
out as an odd, awake poet wets me.
Swimming with large word wings
captured in a net cinched by freedom,
by riveted Caribbean caricatures. Upon
birth from bloody seaweed waters,
fish-
nude. Flap invincible magic. Exist.
Write strong, bend some adverb muscle.
I repeat, write strong. Astonish a monk.
Join the poet parade.
It's storming outside. Not rain,
masturbating kangaroos.

Clem & Dorothy

Opening the bar at 2
I dawdle, cut lemons, limes,
some canned pineapples,
& stock the silver beer coolers.
Drinking a foaming Rolling Rock
bottle I start the giant tape player, snap
on the many lights & a spinning
disco ball. The music is tiny. Daylight
in the high windows bleaches
the colorful bulbs. I check levels
of the hard stuff, slit bags of ice
for the sink under my station.
I push my hand through warmer
bottles to retrieve another icy
one. I place 2 pickled, purple-
dripping eggs on a paper
plate, & a salt-shaker at the
open end of the bar, sit on a
high stool, & eat breakfast.
The beginnings of the world
arrive. Clem & Dorothy are old. Dorothy unties
the thin scarf from her head as Clem slaps a pack
of Salems & a pack of matches in front of them.
I provide a clean glass ashtray.
Clem giggles before ordering
a draft. There are words in his
giggles I don't catch, but
Dorothy slaps his massive
upper arm. Clem giggles
falsetto, odd for his

buffalo size. "I'm dying,
dontcha knows, but I don't
care, there's BEER!" he
yells like Macbeth at open
sky above the ceiling, then
giggles like a weird girl.
Dorothy gulps her gin on the rocks,
shuddering, blinking.

.Jpeg of Hell

Hovering over ice fire
the poisonous angels,
purely Anglo-Saxon,
stretch their rodent wings
under hairy cellophane, spit
frosted morning
sky seeds at the chickens.

They want yr fucking
money, buddy. Peck at
that cold gold soul, raw
consumer. The poisonous angels,
absolutely Amerikan,
twist their serrated chicken beaks
up yr eye-widening cosmological ass.

The Acid Crisps Yr Eyes

You see, my poem is made of
lake glass & water gravity glue

smooth, subconscious sand plank to the moon
where I overhand dead

birds full of ice, stones, rice, &
cheap ignition at amber

waves of armed
government forces

lob purple agonizing
wax bombs upon

thy gorgeous chest flesh
Ginsberg, Allen full of alert without shirt

you see, Amerika
sucks my poem with

fury on its stainless steel
lips so I am a participant.

Scrubbing Amerika
the Beautiful from my

horse-scented
hands with lavender stalks

churning from sea
to sea, held up in lavish defeat,

completes, corrects being a poet
living in the 21st century. As a

poet I always
eat first. Kiss me, hard.

How to Be a Zombie

Turn on the television. It is not a monstrous
technological mind-fucking machine, nor do
corporate-controlled strings pull puppets
thru the glass to meld into our lives & affect
movement in the cities of the world. Turning
the television on is like lighting Las Vegas, bells,
chimes, girls whooping. It is all good. The sun
shines, & it sets. It is constant entertainment.
Watching television is like watching the sky.

Guilt at Night

Yes, the accusation is sexual.
I am sad. I am guilty. I am
dreaming a culpable prelude but don't
recognize it as a prelude yet.
I am abandoned, discarded,
avoided, & hated. I orbit memory
& feel a rapist's premature ejaculation.
I taste Boston ocean & honey cream
flesh stirred like slow, light-liquid
arms of a spiral galaxy. Everything in the green
Atlantic is in the blue sky, hovering mirrors
swim & mesh. I dissolve under furry sand.
Deep-cut gills, rainbow membranes
bubble into stars & a curved trembling balloon
halfmoon. Nobody will look at me. Materialized
at dusk in the summer, I decide to drive downtown.
I don't recall driving nor parking but I'm walking
dark back city streets below a gigantic townhouse
horizon. As rumbling in the city begins
I watch, horrified by excess, the many
windows of the many townhouses
burst & pour out great smoke
cloud-sculpted waves like tight
gray vomit. I realize I'm a
lone survivor, but as mentally crushed
& dispersed as everyone in the buildings.
This is Pompeii, all ash,
the insane towers, this is now.
I am chewing the corners of my

cotton pillow like salty beef jerky.
Waking, & it's really Sunday,
recalling the passionate dream drama
I smile. I am secure. My pillow
is wet. I am alive, & free, on a new
dangerous day.

Magic for a Modern Culture

An amazing knot-trick
thought, undone by mental tightening
is featured inside a spotlit skull mind.

With muddy wrists & eye twists,
surprise shoulder taps swivel
logic & attention.

Diversion, our current
freefall world.
Big Ben knits

soft seconds
around our modern
moon.

The oceanic stage
tide fools
us.

100% silk water
skin pockets fish,
bones, & other ropes.

Miracles spin, sink,
& hide. Go ride a seahorse
neck of s

tonishment.

49

The Dog Is Talking

You have closed our black bathroom
door, waking on a Friday. The dog is
talking from this side of morning
hallway darkness, "Oh, you're awake!
You're up! I'm here! Let's walk
together down the alley in the rain!
I really have to pee! I want to smell
the perfumed places rabbits nibbled!"

He waits like a corked, furred gland
on old carpet. His old claws dig a
gold strip under the door, with alert
ears he listens for yr fingers
on the doorknob. "Oh, hurry
the whole hell up! I think I have
to crouch in wet grasses to shit,
too! I taste milk! I taste chicken!"

Writing the developing physics
occurring simultaneously, I hear
the back door slam shut from
this little 2nd floor room. You're walking
the dog. We haven't yet sd good morning
to each other, nor kissed, nor
smiled. Our dog is so loud. I'll wait
in the kitchen with a coffee, with 3 words.

Today I Finally Say

This can become a sweet
day. I kneel, genuflect, rise
with a face full of sunlight,
to announce: happiness.

So much hell is held back,
what little hell emerges
I easily endure with a
burning firecracker

banana, a blackening banana.
Well, squeeze the hot banana,
squeeze a lard balloon. Leaf
eyes & small, translucent birds,

fuse-ash, street music, rain
memories, rubbery guns,
flow & burst &
crumble.

Cheryl

I imagine you chomping
velvet purple morning-glory flowers
in today's gray sunlight, chewing
off the luxurious cups & swallowing.
Vitamin Z increases the volume
of sarcastic laughter in yr manicured
garden. You have flower breath, sweet
& odd, a troubling lunch. You've
plucked every screwy soft spaghetti
vine wrapped at the bottom of yr
deck. Extreme squirrel cheeks &
wet bits of morning-glories fill
yr face. You, a flower in an orange
sundress, follow shale stepping stones
to the rosebushes. Thorns & blood
mix in yr mouth as you gorge.
Roses taste like cat ears.

April 1st, 2012

My grandfather whistles to
backyard birds, chuckles under a
straw hat, out of the house; returning
musical responses by plying &
twisting photon slabs of human awareness,
blows an odd clarinet made of old Italian blood.
A little, unrealized spit ends a faint lip reed, snaps
a gold, mica beak. Sitting down on the last, black
stair, the big, blue sky & Ellport's surrounding
wooded hills; yr family, brothers, sisters, yr wife,
dead, a son in the ground, tumble-
weed clouds echo various finches, indispensable nicotine
bluejays. Lassoed hawks like wounded, round hound-
dogs. Robins over 40 years ago, exposed nightcrawlers
goo in the dew of yr yard, wearing time-crushed bells,
warble & dance. You laugh
because the birds sing & even with heavy
dentures you sound like a perfect, chirping bird.
A momentary miracle, that's the hook
pointing back, & the hook, all architectural string,
the very pull of physics, is made of orange
mirror water & bits of eye wings. There are
crows in my oily garage of a goddamn head
armed with memory hatchets & black pouches of
anthrax powder. They fly & pepper shit
over me, worms who need sound kisses. I maintain a grandson's
silence so my nauseous soul screams to grip exploding maggot
bubbles, indigestion, acid-reflux rungs,
exhaling to turn the sun, like God &

godless existential problems: cauldrons of
slaughtered infants served as vomit stew.
But you hear rare symphonies above earth
ripple from dripping, drenched canoes of
syrupy feathers & dust-thin, ignitable bones.
Aging is totally about momentary miracles
& temporary instruments, constructs, brain rafts.
Trombone fruit cocks. Baby-flute transcendence, aflutter,
ruffles helium soup edges & live vagina wires. A stirred
woman tastes like natural gas in a soft, concrete cellar.
Hunks of flint & quartz slam sparks & fists of maple branches
rustle into flag shapes. Covert, suicidal cymbals smash
leaves & ant-brained, early flowers. Granular, lavender,
granite snakes crash down from morphed paper trees
beneath pulsing, elastic cords of subatomic LSD light. Breath-
frightening beauty, a momentary miracle, this moment
dissolves oak, elms, walnut, mimosa, pines, Ellport,
life, listening to Lawrence Welk, particle disintegration.
We create, without knowing how, our mirrors & echoes &
mysteries. We repeat the birds.
The birds are smiling. I feel why.
It's April Fool's Day, again & again,
& yr grandson is an old mumbling poet,
again & again,
Grandpa.

Save Me, Aimee

So many gun deaths in the city.
Streets pop. Kids die for a bike.
Fuck you is slapped onto their
gang faces. They're dead
before they ride the decades
into old age resignation. Mothers
are crying in the trees like mourning
doves the size of stone statues. Statues
wearing wet clothes, & with this
humid heat, steam feathers
fluff at the awful sun. Drenched
songs remain, sweet, angry, agonizing,
weeping, woeful, religious songs.
There are too many ironies &
realities, sexual secrets, self-
shortened names, dope dope, loves
in 7th grade, college football teams,
1st-person shooter & bloody video games.
To remember infants, energetic dreams,
their favorites foods. Tragedies
snowball Erie this summer in daylight
& at night – an unstoppable wrecking
ball – pendulum of violence swings
faster & faster. I'm stunned. Excessive
shit is choking every answer to rectify
Amerika's poverty culture. We hook
infants to a descending assembly-line belt,
way down the hole where demons eat
their hearts, replace them with puke.

The puke works as a biological switch.
They communicate like cake
fights. Then there isn't a floor anymore
in their minds. Maybe they can fly.

Self Portrait Drinking Wine

Shirtless on a July night, my ponytail
reaches halfway down my back. Of
course my hairline is halfway up
my skull, & most of my remaining
thin gray hair is translucent to the
skin wrapping what I see as my
toothless face, in glasses & a wild
gray goatee. Sometimes the kids of
Amerika address me as "sir," & that
ain't bad, I like it. Sir – one who's closer
to death. Sir – a little goddamn
respect I've lived thru hell & some
heaven. Sir – you created an anemic
generation who shoved me behind
a counter of bullshit. There are times
I get weird looks, which is fine, probably
appropriate, stiffed by the amount of
change. I apologized a long fucking
time ago for being 15 during Woodstock.
I sincerely believed the country was going
to change for the best, for the best of freedom,
of honesty; well, sorry about that
not being the case today. I was living in a
haze. I AM living in a haze. My ponytail
is a rope to nowhere, death, a lost story.
Amerika naturally rotted, & so have I.
I wear dentures, creak with arthritis,
& smile however I can smile. My ponytail
is a smile, too.

Maybe Baby
(for Bud Backen)

Maybe it's very
sugary black
coffee. Maybe
the poem just
rose from a
nap. Maybe
words require
energy like cars
need melted
dinosaurs. Maybe,
very maybe,
I'm a skin puppet.
Maybe a string-
attached poem
expands my
clown
eyes, a slow
pull from the
wrapped
finger of
Buddha
standing
all dizzy &
swaying &
dangerous. Maybe
Buddha has coconut
sunblock. Maybe
the river

is really
more than
hologram.
Maybe Minnesota
is real.

These Lone Hours

I see Ed Sullivan with a tomahawk
clenched in his teeth. He is very
constipated. On all fours, Ed
is sneaking toward Dean
Martin, who is snoring in a leather
chair. The stratospheric smell of
gin & limes, cigarettes, Tabu perfume
laced with sex juice. Ed Sullivan
is insane, naked as daylight shadow,
filled with murderous fury for no
solid reason, to follow the
funnel of
history.
Death by tomahawk surprise.
It's in my head where Ed
& Dean live & die in the glory of
translucent lunacy.

So this Has Been Morning

Before dawn I down my
pills, prepare coffee, talk
to the cats, call for our
dog to chain him up outside, drip
eye drops, open some curtains.
Ann is already at work.
The house feels hollow
as I enter my small
room to write, armed
with black coffee & my
fingers. Sure, after
throwing words at
poems, I feed the cats
their plates of wet food,
retrieve the beast,
refill my Halloween-scene
cup with good old rock
& roll energy mud. I don't
know how hours fly,
but they fly, & I, still
layered in sleep clothes,
straddle the roll of the
world to sit, tenuous balance,
on top of thin
noon. Oily sky bearings
stick just at
that moment
I begin to
fall into

late, dark day,
defeated by enormity,
by eternity, again.

Flower of Syria

Sitto, you left this brain & soul world in 1985.
Nobody knew yr true age, birth certificates of
women born way back around the beginning
of the 20th century in an obscure village in Syria
did not exist. We knew our grandfather had
come to Amerika with yr older sister, but she
died young, & he traveled back to Syria to
yank you from underneath a table. You were
next in line, it was law. You had no say. It was
awful, but you birthed 4 daughters. A year
before I, the first grandson from you, emerged,
my grandfather died a long, painful death at
the edge of New Castle, Pennsylvania. I never
met him in any form except for molecular
entwining; but you, Sitto, what I remember:
a flower of unconditional happiness,
the smiling flower of Syria. Love.

Lesions of Knowledge

We know what happened to invoke the loss of honeybees. Pressed against a piece of Lake Erie, a key section of land in 21st-century upper Pennsylvania, where poisoned atoms hook & tango with fresh, molecular sisters of air: pesticides. Sheets of pesticides spread across decades of grape-fields & farmlands killed a large portion of flourishing honeybees. Human poison. A nightmare ballet of swirling, sand-like, scissoring clouds. The dance between ingenuity & murder. Grapes or infected grapes. Insecticide. Invasive insects. Bastard insects chew the leaf, thus, we solve that issue with invention. An intention to drive honeybees to extinction wasn't a part of the plan; nonetheless, such events occur after we strive for solutions against the natural world & its pests, innocent life-forms choke. I swear I remember more butterflies existing, bats, gnats, & grasshoppers, walking-sticks, more wasps, a wider array of birds. I feel an insistence is specific to a loss. I used to have long, black hair. Internal pain was diluted by the light of life. Soaked words like socks in soup, a bone spoon, now spin.

The vacuum of disaster. Once rich with paramecium, dull tap water. Sun burns edges of atmosphere hair, sizzling, curling short, buffeting the sky with fire. We live in the calcified future world created by the dead. The buzz, the buzz-cut, the buzz-saw, the buzzards & crows. Sucking straws stuck into eyeballs, honey thins to pale mucous & static renditions of silence. Sip the bubbles of pesticide drift.

Seeing from the Eyes on Each of His Fingers
(for Jeff Filipski)

His fuck fingers cross over his heart as he sleeps
knocked out by blood rum & cactus juice in the
ocean. One bare foot on a porch plank, the hammock
weeps & screams, which rustles Jeff's siesta. The beach
is packed with cartoon characters tuned to reggae &

coconut drums. Every male is one-third boner. By blink-
ing seagulls intestines are tossed off a pier on a moonless
midnight, plus rainbow paper confetti flies. Globular
renditions of semen the size of cats jump at the
sky hole of all spiritual travel, then his 12 hands ache

from clawing at dark hours. To at least bring blood. Look,
men need houses on their shoulders, & women shld have
tits the size of moons filled with maple syrup & arsenic.
Everybody is drunk tonight, except the kids, & some of
them are stoned. A hut leans from its insistence to curve.

Above a blue rock deep in the greenest vegetation gravity
completely fails somewhere at the edge of Florida. Along
with blood & oxygen, visions made by paint receptors
adjust his huge skeleton & muscular structure
to twirl into a black, backyard garage & relate

the moment expanding with the surreal & hallucinatory
reality. That moment before reality occurs one senses
reality. But cut that floor out, &
drop. Drop acid. Drop bats like pepper over the black

mountains. Drop yr drawers & dance. Drop yr pants &

freeze, fill with modesty whoops, too late. Filipski has
been here playing inside nightmares like R. Crumb &
redemption is too late. It's fine, relax, we're
past all that unnecessary
zen shit.

On Such a Clear Blue Sunny Sunday

Let's get the fuck you out of the way. Fuck
you packed on a coconut beach, fuck you
beer-drunk in a boat on Lake Erie

with yr tanned happiness the sun
burns on yr face like a smile at
death. That's all the way the hell

you go, I guess, the edge of death.
Then what? I'm all hollow & bored
& everybody is a dead fish lapping

up on the seaweed pebbles, staying.
The nauseous aquatic breeze
blows across the city. The great OM

of an ecstatic hermit
has been nibbled & chomped
into verbal skylight growling

fuck you at me in a sweaty room.

I Tell You

I tell you a photon's
journey from the center of
the sun to its surface takes

150,000 years. "How do
scientists know that?" you
scoff. I tell you they

have studied the sun.
They have insane telescopes
& see things thru different

light spectra, gamma,
x-ray, more, to the
core. They *know*. It is

factual physics, I tell you.
"So what?" you reply.
"It has nothing to do

with everyday reality."
Yeah, but, I remember,
I grow silent, a mute photon,

King Crimson's album
cover of a red
scream. I tell you

subatomic particles

by nature, exploded,
are paradoxical

beauty & mystery.
"Sweetheart, that means
nothing, nothing at all."

I tell
you –
exactly.

Leaning against the Wind

After 30 years in the factories,
muscularity. I hit 7 years this week
working in a pod at a computer
with a phone company, 7 years
from the union strike. Did my
time by the burn barrels watching
dawn curl orange & black over
dew-wet trees, holding a picket sign.
Then a new job with a headset
talking to all of Amerika from a
chair. In these 7 years my muscles
are gone, but I'm not dead nor
so pissed off at daily existence
I flip like an ape off a cliff
of breath, or sanity. Oh,
I have flipped away from sanity,
true.
Like an ape.

I Have Nothing To Say

I have nothing to say because there is so much fire & radiation.
I have nothing to say as a smoldering lamb wraps upon my head.
I have nothing to say in the face of erupting hell-fire spontaneity.
I have nothing to say about mangled steering arms, charred tie rods.
I have nothing to say with steamy Jupiter visible before cold dawn.
I have nothing to say about the 21st century & Negative Capability.
I have nothing to say against injustice, especially in the flame arts.
I have nothing to say that a black dog is a cellular, green feline
clutching wires over Raspberry Street like a hooked, gasoline balloon.
I have nothing to say to defend vacuous innocence. I have nothing to
say
to you tho we, match-sticks, talk. I listen & I have nothing to say to
deny
time is satanic metaphor. I have nothing to say engulfed in hot,
impeccable
light, showered with a ton of lava ink. I have nothing to say from
a future human base on Mars, dust coats my tongue. I have nothing
to say, hunched inside a cave 10,000 years ago. I have nothing to say
but that the bread is ash. The bread is ash. The goddamn bread is ash.

1,000 Balloons

then 10,000 balloons
then 100,000 balloons
cross the Pacific

follow hugging airflow
above the
clouds 1,000,000 balloons

filled with various
deadly viruses
& ignited eggs of white powder

rain-pollen &
bacterial sky-dust ignorant
gnats chop with machetes.

Utter madness
sifts over
everything Amerikan.

1,000 balloons
& vast multiplications
occur daily, en masse,

as cloaked invisible
stars under the clouds burst
eternal, curved, helium mist,

unscrubbable air,

doom, & audible echoes
from death. All

the neighbors
are sparkling &
infected.

Triassic Tuba

I think I see my
high-school girlfriend,
Kathy, smiling like a partial
Buddhist. The Beatles &
the Rolling Stones entwine
their sticky DNA inside us.
We live in the land of the holy
free – free to say hell no. Free
as air & the stars & thought.
There are not walls lining
our horizon. Burr names me
Andy. Billy calls me Andy.
Nobody else equates me with
an Andy. Burr is now dust &
Billy is a mayor. Kathy dissolves
under swishing, oceanic decades.
Tacked to facts, medicinal spirits.
Gooseberries are lightly furred while
worms rise for warm, afternoon rain.
Fire rings the poles, licks Buddha's
rubber belly, burns the translucent finger
of Jesus. Science is the weight of a single
soul. With damaged wings we descend.
With slit throats songs pulse as they
pour into silent, feathery history.
Coins & flames spray from a golden,
volcanic tuba we know as the real
world. Existential terror trumps
art. I think I see

high-school dinosaurs
breeding, confused by music &
time.

Singing on the Stairs of the Years

Hold that stance, sitting on the top step.
Arms crossed like salamis, fingers twisty
with anxiety. Stop, freeze, let the smile
drip. Sadder. The saddest poet in Amerika
sunlit on the top stair. Good. Good. Now
go ahead & do with yr face what you
want. I'm snapping one hundred & twenty
a minute. Beautiful, that snarl. What
are you doing? Do it, baby. Yr hair
smells like a spicy poetry
stew full of carrots & aromatic
urinals in theaters. Wet goddess
suck – the perfect picture. Don't
hold.

Thinking of Another Poem

Pumpkin beer, hell the fuck yes,
in the middle of September in
the center of afternoon, wearing
green shorts & no shirt, green-tinted,
dark-plastic, new glasses, & a long, gray,
thin pony-tail. Sitting in a brown chair
at my little, upstairs desk's laptop,
writing this poem as directly as nailing
spikes into a fat, stripped tree. The sun,
God, the sun, it is a monster. It is obscene.
It is horrific. It is ignorant I have a little,
soft, feather soul. I have a hammer
forehead made of pumpkin pulp.

Waking from Two Nightmares

Uncle Duke tackles a wounded hyena.
The hyena hums "Mr. Tambourine Man"
as it rolls, slow-motion, in lush foliage with
Uncle Duke hugging its back legs, & it can't
snap teeth at his arms. The hyena's
jaw is broken, swings like a heavy, fur hinge. I
know my eyes are opening before dawn
& I know I am not Bob Dylan. I realize
Uncle Duke has been deceased for several
years, but the symbolic hyena? Hell if I know.
I rise to piss & to wonder why I'm seeing
Uncle Duke, at all, in my dreams. Do ghosts
throw molecules into the rivers of our brains?
It's 3:30 in the frigid morning. I'm thinking
about the dead, my mind is flying for the light,
so I turn for a sleeping pill before I return
to our bed where Ann's rhythmic snore
of breath while asleep smells of old, distant
milk. I turn my face on the black pillow &
listen. I hear daylight. Ann is gone to work.
It's snowing like yesterday, yet it's colder.
I feel tackled in my bedclothes drinking
chilly coffee, wrapped by poems &
imagined scream laughter.

When Are You You?

To question a momentary face
in a momentary mirror I hold
years like hot scorpions made
from mercury ingots & granite
fleck poison in my hands.

Oxygen cake starred by hydrogen candles.

Exploding time water.

Early deaths. I did not die.
Why survive when
stung by the force of sharp
poison? I understand I have always
been a jointed name to skin &

bone. You? Are you fucking
linear, seriously? Have you
grown in the guts of a flower
womb to burst egg
seeds? Obviously. Did you

swallow? There is no yes
since everything alive is
naturally yes, plus storms in a
desert. Plus long insane days
of creepy deafening sunlight.

A leaking teen. A chancy

but viable infant. Tarry
arterial blood. Snap veins
open now; pop, enlarge,
become the memory of scorpions.

Bumbles

The cat licks
her fence-shadow
side, blind as a
pressed-together
tunnel. "Miss
Kitty-lips," Ann
sometimes
calls
her. A pure Disney
princess gone
real & above
everyone in the world.
She is curled on a red
pillow. A few hours
occur as actual mist
while really raining all day.
Gray film light
pockets our tired city.
Bumbles, the cat curled
on a red pillow,
yawns below the window.
Terrifying fin teeth.
White pyramid needles.

Poets Age

I don't think we have decades.
5 years, 3 years,
1 year? Tomorrow
when the atmosphere
splits like a corduroy pistachio
& all atomized oxygen
rushes through that
cracked hole? Rapturous.
But CNN staff are plain
dead & blue, & we won't
even get to see that end shit.

List incredible diseases
& fears of diseases & possible
diseases. Old people, biological
eventuality. What lungs?
What brain-withered sanity?
From the wet loop of time
from a swampy womb mother
is a girl we swim out of a girl
to die. We compose carbon
ghost poems for fleshy
light beings eons from earth birth.

Soul Repair

The first inhalation splits
hydrogen between my nostrils.
A cleaver of skin shines
on the tip center of my infant nose.
As I inhale smoking rag-dolls &
ignited tentacles, the pulsing moment;

oxygen button-eyes pop off
to create today's spewing morning,
& a wet man rolls like a deeply-peeled
apple over nuts of crushed sky.
Paramecium granules
remain. Step between the sounds

of bone & stone discourse. Be a monolith
made of phosphorescent jellyfish & soft
fish fingers, blue sugar, to block echoes.
No subatomic particle pierces
further inside the goo, I am composed
of amber syrup & hallucinations, breath.

It Can't Be Night

I look at the blue clock. Today
my closet door is green, fresh,
3 coats of paint. Plus the cellar
steps are swept, granules of
feline litter, fur, muck, crossings
of spider webs sticking to a
straw broom; gas-man comes,
I let him inside, get our mail.
Eat 2 chicken sandwiches.
There are always miscellaneous
acts, too, interspersed between
the hours, the slow spin, things.
For instance, talking to Ann
about writing. My daughter
returns my call. Bringing an
empty orange crate back into
my room. Ann does laundry. All our clothes
are old clothes. Belts I buy from
Kmart rip after a short while. My stomach
grows & recedes, grows & recedes,
42" to 36", 40" to 38",
weird. Where did today go?
Who was I? What did I do? Like
hell in a basket, fire flares
from a casket, & not in India.
Necessity, triangulating place &
time, calling it another blood day.
The holy spot our minds are planted
in cake yolk sod. The crushed egg

rain is almost snow from gray
sky cloud feathers. Immensity,
intrinsically, is a feathery sledgehammer.
I live a little life, paint a door green,
breathe the air of Erie, Pennsylvania
as evening drops like a stunned
nun. What is believed is real.
Then we dream underneath black
black sleep capes.

All this Temporary Bullshit

Acorn walls, the water bill, my
Halloween coffee cup; Sunday
morning rain. Old, tarry fog, our
dog with his name, blue dust falls
under my wrists; Alice orbits
the moon. Girls, old as women,
pack on clay makeup, Egypt
their gray eyes, straighten wig skulls.
Boys, who are natural jackhammers,
chew chunks of flint bedrock,
shake without control in deep chairs,
stirred by eternal, circular dementia.
Deaths increase like eels in black grease.
The trees are sand & sawdust & ghostless.
I write to think a poem grows fangs to hook to
eyeball gelatin.

Bela

Bela Lugosi sleeps here. Witches
wiggle headfirst out his nostrils,
cackle before their afterbirth
slops from the plugs of curled feet.

Bela doesn't flinch, nor do his dreams
alter the flow of gamma rays & micro-
waves the witches brew & blow
across the Alps & black lakes. Rain

contains cold blood. Pharmaceuticals,
evil intentions. Bela allows absolution
to thin, thin as a translucent
oak wafer. As witches accumulate

capes around his ankles in salty water,
Bela belches the sweet taste of opium
like a word for inevitable horror.
Sound asleep, Bela believes in Buddha

bubbles. Cocaine coconuts roll
down gray clouds. Mr. Lugosi,
less lung from the long burp,
sighs & sniffles. Life is always
correcting mythology.

January 2

Snow, tons of ice flakes globe
our plebeian, pyramidal world.
Winds cut west. Sky, gray eggshell blur.
The adventures of new 2014:
neighbors' growling snowblowers:
prehistoric soundwaves twist, cha-cha-cha,
tango dip, & do the Fukushima radiation fish
with all the curvy fingers & arms & noses
of groovy winter trees in the city. Between
exhales of Monk, breathy, uranium sirens.
Inhaling, his golden soul from our living room
undresses my ear skin, & I feel silenced by
listening to wheeled engines eat knee-deep
snow. Coin the size of my hand inside a
black, flat machine downstairs, but upstairs
the machine ascends, armed, alarmed,
dancing like chained wheels on the cold, cold moon.

There Are No Surprises

It is yr birthday today. We talked
about no gifts, no cards,
for these 3 consecutive days of
yr birthday, Valentine's
Day, & our 10th actual,
er, not actually, marriage
anniversary. We agreed
to just kick back & forget
it all. I remember in the past
our similar agreements
never held tight – I'd
surprise you at work
with a delivered bouquet,
whatever else occurred.
This the first year I really
mean there are no surprises
or amber earrings or
Fedex flowers or store cards,
not even a restaurant reservation.
We go for our eye examinations
Wednesday, new glasses,
that counts for something.
Hell, we've
given each other our soul,
our experience in
time & days. You do
all kinds of things for me,
& likewise, always. I am
utterly grateful you were

born. I love you,
with the fury of the cosmos,
forever. There are
no surprises.
See the light of the sky?
That's me, that's you.

Sunday

Breath of milk & sleep
dreams to wake you
are you awake? I repeat
three big times prone
with you in our black
bed, & yr hhmmm? is
a flower opening before
dawn, a soft occurrence in a
stone, toothless world. You
rise for our animals on the
other side of our door,
& I blink & I think & do
not try to fall back into
sleep, I'm wide awake.
The world is go. Atoms
smash as strange, violet
sunrise severely darkens
window shadows. Soon curtains
burn crisp butter, all this
smoke from thought. Roll
up, get to the beginning,
roll into noon with
hands full of marbles
the size of floating hours.

Repeating Miracles

Clocks
fill with choking swamp water & numbers
on the clock face become curled seahorses
who sneeze like a cursive word. Their
main evolutionary form of locomotion.
Clocks erupt.
Seahorses grow wet snakeskin wings made of
old echoes & the feel of the past. Peeling memory
from personal history, the mutated seahorses
surface with horrible burning effervescence.
Seahorses kiss before water boils.
Seahorses bob under mountainous clouds
south of the lake like specks of balloons.

Another Picture

The dog barks like an elephant
submerged in a cave of blood.

Baby-blue trucks suck the skin limbs
of deflating drivers. These weird dawn

reflections occur upon a moist
surface of dirt. We announce leaf

has noise. We grow oval windows from
the ends of our fingers & toes & lips.

Poems. Cricket dew. Tiny birds. The
eventual spin in the heart of a wild onion.

Tango days of doors.
Ejaculate crashes thru glass centuries

odored by iron. Green rust mosses over
a womb. A purple, glandular, embryonic

dragonfly with a name. He hovers like
cinnamon in the morning above strong

coffee. A lifetime is lashed to an
oxygen pendulum. Walking trees,

we people think. We think thru decades.
We are atomic players. Hydrogen & helium

93

linebackers after the proton snaps.
Our movie nebula

burns
in the wind of the sun.

Packed inside an acorn, quantum
antelopes

wake, bristle their natural fury
with slices of orange melon teeth.

Dragonflies made of molecules & viruses.
Antelopes are full of clawing monkeys.

Whatever our mouths say,
a zoo of tragedy.

Existence requires
tragedy.

Locusts inside Morning Oak Trees

There must be uranium under all the summer
leaves, beneath slaughtered roses as infested beetles
chew thru that aromatic world.
A total clicking fuck you from a Geiger counter
bathed in skylight & impending cloud shadow.
Uranium teeth eat our feet.
Uranium leaks odd fog wisps from the grass.
Uranium burns the hair from the face
of a photographed cat.
Uranium ascends its poison
ankle-level – where bumblebees are cigarette ash.
There must be uranium radiation
infecting the city of Erie today.
Too many crows sound horrified.
Too many Raspberry Street cars growl while
dropping into a hole of incredibly deep echoes.
Locusts, unaffected, sheet the awful contamination.
Uranium blows dandelion brain cells at a day moon.
Live with it.

Self Portrait as a Space Emissary Alien

Every atom has been something. Laptop
key contains the nausea of Wallace
Stevens. Beneath years of fingered indentations
the orgasmic ecstasy of Christ. Wiggling Hitler
microbe bubbles goo. An Egyptian & a pyramid.
Sitting Bull offers berries of light from
his astonished existence. The space bar's
molecules. A brontosaurus trombone slides
pieces of Peru. Ungodly pity, taboo visions,
scotch breath of Pope Paul the 12,000[th].
The wet leaf, a lamp with an illegal incandescent
bulb. A yodeling Yankee is an orange cupcake crumb.
Mastodons fuck on a snowy evening, their silhouettes
shake. Einstein swirls in cigar smoke with formulas &
his deathbed smile. Peasant piss & hawk shit.
There are billions of birds in one small white candle.
My bones have squid & odd marine life in them.
My blood was granite fever, masked psychopaths, cave fire.
The Statue of Liberty armed with secret high-tech
weaponry. Embarrassed hippo snot.
Joyous vultures. Ocean bag over the shoulder of Santa.
Cannibals eat & puke & eat & puke, eat puke.
The gears of the government
turn, but those loud wheels scream like torture
echoed in a low-ceiling street maze. Forays
out the door, into the gray air with confused
intentions. The clerk was a blast of ash
licked up by a rat who spins.
Lice sneeze

to achieve nirvana. Fishing in the greenest
green water. Hooking
bait words. Word. Worm rockets. Tree-sized blood
missiles connect to humans.
Earth's arctic ice is preparing for
action.
Time will be so very taffy & dangerous.

Self Portrait as Mask

I have been tempted to tear
everything from my writing-room walls,

but not in the vicious, insane manner
when I left my previous house

wounded, slaughtered by divorce.
A sane erasure to white

nicotine walls of harmless paper monsters.
I wish my eyes were green, or blue, or teal;

Oriental, Mayan, perfectly
Egyptian, or square as laptops.

This nose, clumped in fat DNA hands
of Syria & Italy, cold & red &

large: shrink it, tone it, slice it way
down. I want to choke Jimmy

Durante to death with his
Ahh cha-cha-cha-cha acceptance of

apathy. Maybe I'm the son of
a long-eared Texan, a bitch beagle. Scissor

meat gristle a good 6 inches around
each ear. All my lost teeth,

they swoop from heaven & plant their
roots, rejuvenated, back into my jawbone.

As for the crispy, rose-petal poems
inside my skull, crush them

in a mortar into fine powder &
snort the dark lines. Dream freedom

bells
ring.

Dream
Man Ray

dies &
a small mirror

sucks
his face.

A yoga calendar
curls into a triangle.

I'm
nude, again.

Self Portrait as Cyclonic Interruption

My nipples are bugged. My lips crust –
split. Wet sandwich eyeballs, egg stage.

I am a lone, startling, majestic mammal maggot
haloed inside geodesic, prismatic thought mirrors.

Man-manipulated skylight warps my art as orange
as the fury of Zeus' piss soaked with nicotine. Patina

of old veined phones. There are scissors all
over my echoes. Resonance becomes my personal faceted

jewel. Bones sud to detergent & the ionosphere pulls
my bubbles. My circular aspirations

hammer the blood-bloated clouds.
Worms fall like paint & fumes ascend.

Sledgehammer satellites
crush aluminum-foil time with a billion

volts of radio. They orbit my mind.
Extract entire segments of life. Introduce

the process of injected death. My beard is
wired. Words wing to iridium

pendulums. Secrets like dumped cement
plant my neck. The radiated scythe of evilness

glints as it swings across angular river
conspiracy. My skull smile is actually upside down.

We Burn to Pledge

A toad jumps but only the split skin of the toad
jumps. Flags of schools burst into fire & student
skulls roll in boiling blood-streams along curbs.
Jaws crack off like fresh, crushed walnut shells
under flaming tons of wheels. Long ghosts hook
bottom echoes, pull at hems & breasts of dreams.
Bone ash pyre smolders where a yellow bus crashes.
Imagine yellow buses. Inherent insanity of DNA slides
like Halloween lava over black concrete plates &
filleted erasers. The weight of the moon is the
weight of ash plus you, squared by algebra. Faint from
freedom. History needs burning twigs, electrocuted elephants,
& chalk minds. We test kids to limit pliability & political
revolution. A buzzard circles a devastated land.
An asbestos-cloaked figure kneels over
a charred piece of flag. A flashing car is a poisoned
fedora locked onto the head of a damaged sheriff.
Realize enlightenment is more necessary than education.
Existential culpability, glandular secretions, fuck finger aware,
holiday memories, Hollywood heroin, our system of social sin.
Skeletons of myopic, overwhelmed teachers
scream instructions over excavating fires. Their bones expand
& float away with smoke-fat waves of nuclear devastation.
Every kid is deaf & dead. Every desk, the flushed janitor.
Melted clocks. Books, properties of rooms & halls &
historical lies splinter in tumbling winds
across the uneducated land.

Burning on Mercury

Fusion & fire
endless sheets of radiation
we whistle happy tunes

*

Another noon-blue lamb
crosses a dissolving methane bridge &
announces yr name backwards

*

Heat expands
flowers heart yr eyes
nuclear war parents die

*

Puppets, my old string bones
sun muscles an attitude
be wood

*

Earthlings
snow forms around bone particles
this is really Kansas

*

Buffaloes chew our hair
buffaloes ignite like gasoline igloos
buffaloes roam this baked land

Come up against the Last Inhalation

I am tired. Bubbling for decades
against ceiling surface where water
meets precise swords of air slicing
mammalian, oxygenated indoctrination
from cold blood & no eyelids & a murky
world. A distinct point, human
poetry weaves wetness & a parched existence.
The flesh ascends as wood, as
rock, as rubber balloon following rules of
natural physics. Is this moss? Is this hair? Is
my nose a failed fin? Fresh lake cut by a
final glacier's stretching reach, its fingertips
claw into hot oatmeal cliffs. A great lake
I curl in my throat to name by syllable.
After all this time & timelessness I
simply think without words.

These Things Happen

I blow quartz dust off the wings
of a blood orchid after discovering
I'm locked in a sunroom without
fists or a phone. Spider plants spill
water in the shape of snake tongues
rusted over green iron. Flowers, colors,
leaves, stems, the flesh of petal, wet,
natural, floral clarinets. Fly-eye windows.

Seroquel. Motion-sensing mind kaleidoscope.
A woman with blue butter hair insinuates past
attacks, altho she's a flash scene in an old bus dream.
I swallow handfuls of wet opals from an onyx bowl.
The stone floor softens like blood mud.
It's astonishing & alarming, bird songs & no birds.
Voices from hallucinated people. Things
I must do in a wrap-around sunroom on the bay.

Killing Spiders

To distinguish wood from bone a female spider
laces echoes with listening. Sight like a rain of bats.
My love's jaw hinge is made of sonar &

rusty sanity. Sun dust. Skin cells. Insect atoms.
Visual memories of feelers crunch the last
years of Miles Davis. Her multiple eyes slide

into my one eye, elastic gamma vision. Beneath
skin her spider ghosts swim with mermaid skeletons.
Cars are painful wailing walruses in poisoned light.

Necessity crisps emotional crust. Candle trees.
Hellish, spiritual complications occur after
the brightest fire. She blinks in a bouncing web.

Driving from a Floating Position

Ghosts laugh like cowboys riding oily

carburetor atoms. Fanged dash-light lambs.

Red poison flames pulse. Reptilian moneymen

pound blunt broken thigh bones onto the dust of

Mars & thru packed, microbial streets of Earth.

High-hat flaring cymbals of the sun.

Snares string necklace cash & visual echoes. There are more

articulations than chords. Flesh,

odor of wet rugs. Old moldy folded dogs.

Skin ash after napalm. Exoskeletons hold

foggy yard childhood visions & radio voices.

Our destinations are clock erasures.

I Was Going to Say Something

Milk in my eyes.
I wear a maple tree tie.

Shuffle headstone shoes across
dew. Variations

lose centers. Deer silence
before a comma sprints & zigzags.

Deer silence listens. A poem
sodomizes a feeding mosquito.

A poet is a feeding mosquito.
A poet is a comma hooked under a

doe at dawn.
Buckshot bullets spray

into wood & crisp leaves.
I sign my name with finger fog.

Manifesto against Light

We become the timeless world. Edges of
edgeless electrons, porous molecular soup.
We are the world with Tennessee trombones
made of syrup & cigarette smoke. Our
hands drip eyeball pyramids.
Protozoa wiggle in bone marrow. We
are the world. Flesh or ash, bone or cloud.
Mounting tonnages of soul.
Gray autumn sky eyes. Balloons fill with
bells & pour from every smile of dog &
octopus. Reddening oak trees, the sheer
relief of defeat. We become
a wasp's wing at the bottom of a windowsill.
We reverse sunsets on Mars. We are the
world with moonshine tales punctuated by
crickets the size of black elephants in the trees.
Our jellyfish feet slime over gravel.
Congressional disintegration. The glint of a
bomb.

I Was Thinking

Rules of the games are always changing. Penelec
receives a 16% increase. More darkened
houses in this shadowy cold city on a great lake.
Those with less.

Hundreds of dollars
for repairs of bodies &
minds, & no medical insurance.
No goddamn money.

They have us all by the balls. They always
have. We have our life movies.
We have our epiphanies.
Micro-implants. Flags.

Blood tests. Inoculations. Our hands
absorb our hearts
in a morning
classroom.

Ball Equals Equation

I have tasted dust of a baseball
diamond. In a muddy parking lot,
tire tracks fill with tadpoles – tiny
Loch Ness monsters weave the top
of milky coffee in the summer of '65.

There's a rut in my brain. I'm
behind a weak backstop. Copperhead
coils on a stump, I heave a big rock
to crush it. Applause of God & locusts
rushes thru treetops. An

eternal,
internal
moment. I crush
the snake dead
behind the fencing before

I become an old, calculating man.
Between the ghost of that crushed
snake & a thousand noisy
rectifications logically salted & aged,
I am planted. Spiked to a subatomic

crucifix in
time, spinning in mud mutilation.
To get wood, to crack a ball 100 yards.
To get a long stretched-
web catch at the edge of this elastic life.

Movement in a Corner

Clear blue sky light. Not a muscle
of leafless trees flexes until I notice
ends of maple twigs are moving by
subtle pulsations of atmospheric spin.

Photons are pulled from frosted rooftops.
It's such a still, frozen morning, tho atoms
shake maracas & yelp
with open arms to welcome quarks like

ghosts filtering thru live cells. The fog of
gray electrons eaten by blue sky
light. Molecular taffy. Quarks
snowball over the world.

Callouses, skin under skin, skull
under sky, ice in the alley;
defenseless. A supersonic star
screams at us, but we don't hear it.

I listen to a dog bark, old jazz
playing downstairs, huff of our
furnace blowing magical heat
on a cold, quiet December morning

drinking coffee made of crushed
mud beans soaked in blood. A liquid
target is also innocent as a culpable
creation. Miniature chimpanzees

pop off my fingernails, dive
for the laptop's hard-drive jungle.
Hooked, the wasp-colored face
of an ape weighs down my bearded

jaw.

Lemons

Lemons injected with
gasoline shine. Lemons drip
Tuesday dew on the moon.
Lemons liquefy lucidity.
Lemons bob in a lumbering
dinosaur footprint.
Lemons scatter from a hose
of chlorine gas, squirt gnats big
as Grape-Nuts tossed like scattered
grenades at the sun. Lemons
instead of sex teeth.
Lemons not dirty dreaming eyes.
Lemons roll off the
slope of Durante's nose.
Lemons float over watery
gravity graves in a dark storm.
Lemons leak sour rain, swirly cloud
rinds, yellow dust, & terrible decisions.
Lemons crush blood bags
at altars of the seriously hypnotized.
Levitating lemons buoy across
Christ's spiked palms like alien orbs.
Lemons wiggle their slick seeds into
soft fruit eggs. Lemons ovulate &
detonate a spray of eventual
apple-breath sighs.

Crazy Lunar Chickens

Seriously, Amerika
has no bases on/in the
moon? The hidden vultures
of war & death – hollow, spacious,
a surprising egg. Aiming
yolk-colored laser missiles shot
out of crazy lunar chickens.
Amerikans
love moonlight &
superiority,
a chicken-ass ace in space.

What to Remember

I've been writing poems all this time.
I've been stupid, there is no money
to bequeath. I discover bones of
moonlight prop the sky like a bent tent.
I smell serious wealth. A foggy gold
night rain. Look around, but words
are less than coins on every level below
imagination. I know broke.
I know bliss.

Fish Like

Worms whistle
across shards of Mars.
From lips of volcanoes
an opaque hook hovers,
engineers another satanic
digital book. All cats lose
gravity by sectional
moments in dusk light.
Applaud rainbow trout
with arms made of lake mud.
The sun is increasingly unstable.
Dark energy grunts.
We are pulled into pulsing atmosphere
& barbs of oxygen under
dusty water. We inhale grubs &
tadpoles & assholes & visions
of Mars.

Green Light Unison Symphony

Shot up a tube rushing oxygen,
a suck is recognized by yr ears &
shoulders. Then the air spins
& lifts & it's been minutes.
Drop & roll on mattresses
on the grassy moon.
What a ride.
A fun future as a military
killer. Every human forgives you.
The alien creatures have no
philharmonic soul. They have
slow bounding boulders,
no eyes & no musicals.

Get up off Yr Ass

I command my brain to
say

get up off yr
ass

feed the cats, check the list
of things to possibly do.

A flat Monk circle
up the stairs

right thru my green
door

where I
write poems on the

internet.
Poetic pesticides

spray down the curve
of the bone world.

The sun burns
future consumers.

Hot glass
freezes culture.

Time
ash vanishes.

The human race
is cemented to death

holes
ants rush up.

Another One of those Mornings

Dawn rain has become middle morning
snow. Waking in the bathroom mirror,
an old man's face. I ingest my repairing
medicines, put on my glasses, insert my teeth,
avoid a 2nd glance at the mirror. I know
what I look like, nothing pretty
about decay. I am drinking a whole
horse of coffee. A sliver of God
from over 4 billion years ago is implanted
inside my brain. I think about the taste
of eggs, not nourishment. I used to eat
scrambled eggs & raw chopped onions,
a delicious lift; my guts say no
to that now. No raw chopped onions.
Let's paint over our mirrors, sweetheart.
Let's not. Let's kiss. Let's not know our own
faces. Let's ring our ears with cut onions.

Leaping to Say Hello

Slithering around word-pits, worm-pits,
horned maggots slide with gray honey
flooding from a broken skull. The final
crack against plasterboard culture, a poetic
fainting & falling to a dusty carpet. Pulling
at worms with arm claws, I swim like a
square, splintered monolith, sinking. Dead
people have created most of the world we
know, & they don't personally give a
shit. The lion's teeth, lilacs. It's
all about sensory enhancement.
There are streets & windows realigning
air as reality on the other side of the back door.
Air, a poem with breath soothes with
hope, denying
time.

Swiss Acid

An acid night in Switzerland
is inhaling turban sparkles
grape & red grape & red galore
bulbs swirl to the peaks of Lugano.
An echo's edges door lush brick alleys.
Twenty-some fingers & two heads of us
emerge like turds from the ass
of a tropical butterfly moon. We
climb into our pulsing underground villa
in 1973. I hear The Doors Dennis
blasts in his padded headphones.
Like her hair, like her fractured mind,
all of Darlene's clothes are ripped,
yet she laughs mute tripping on the
dorm room floor. Dennis smiles her way.
Jim Morrison cums on the ceiling,
drips snarling red-eyed owls.
Indians who vomit rabbits.
Stairs made of black whiskey flow.

Cannabis Cartoons

In 1970 I hear dump trucks on the moon gear
& smoke – sniff oil-mist lace in
the sky. Clogs my nose, a stuffy water-dripping
moose. Sneezing like a shocked pug. Listening,
a tuned wren is coated by amber tar droplets

as Jay thumbs the roach back. Parked by the
Big Beaver River at the edge of a cliff
in my purple '65 Mustang. All windows
down. Jay plays bass guitar in our
garage band. His giggles climb to falsetto.

His hair is a mop of Tesla's wires.

*

Dave insists it's GOOD hashish. Dave is
in my shop class. Mr. Hammond is near-
sighted in the cellar of
Ellwood City High School. We back

into shadows of anxious cigarettes & smoked
happiness. We bang things with old ballpeen
hammers in a former coal-storage room.
Mr. Hammond never smiles. A lens

on his glasses is cracked at an angle.
He's disgusted at the world.

In this watercolor, I'm holding
a hit of hash in my lungs & my skull is opening

like a drawbridge made of fresh cake.
Dave grins by the light of a dirty window.
This is our last class at the end
of a spinning day.

Migration

I've listened to
a million birds
singing at dawn
while walking out
the factory doors.
They
burn & scream.

Geese, holy & haunted,
shit green-shelled
ice cream cones,
landmines
I twist around
on my work boot
heels.

Poem for the Workers

Amos is a god.
I'm surprised he doesn't realize
running the 600-ton press

is physically handling
a TON of mix & parts.
A couple THOUSAND pounds.

No,
few men can
do the job. Amos has done it

for decades.
He's had all the assholes
as his work helpers.

If Amos doesn't originally
break you he'll
eventually break you.

Few men
can do the
job as helper on the 600-ton.

I was Amos' helper
10 years ago
& now I run the same press.

I have survived

ridiculous scum
helpers, too.

I owe
pieces of shit total hell.

Amos is
a
god.

In 15 Days

Judy retires in 15 days. She's been
counting down aloud since 30.

Her car is inspected for another year.
Her work clothes are tattered & waiting

for the fire. She's got everything
ready & she's got plans:

the son who lives with her in a Lake
City trailer will pay half the bills now.

Otherwise she'd have to live on four
dollars a month.

So she hands Keith a list & he doesn't
say a word. I envision Judy in 1972

with 3 boys
in a Lake City flat. She works two full-

time jobs.
Then the flat burns down

& they lose everything but the
clothes on their backs. The boys'

father never offers
to help them get back on their feet.

Judy drove a Harley.
Judy smoked pot. She wears

pot-leaf earrings to work
to prove it.

She LOVED beer.
She was crew leader

at the Marx Toys factory.
Drove jitney at Niagara Plastics

& raised those 3 boys
on her own. In 15 days Judy

retires & I might
cry. I'll never

see her
again.

Check

Poets never tell you what they are
doing, nor what happens because
of their actions. Packed all around
a poem, between words, glorious, pulseless
silence. I don't mean the loss of language.
Reality isn't English, nor human,
nor is a poet a box of water in the rain. Poets
veer from exposing facts from vanity because
gravity inhales bleached chromosomes thru
nets poets throw on beaches. They
twist in a chair like a crumbling cupcake
crushed across a messy floor.
Poets shout NOUN, VERB, PARADIDDLE,
BLUE SKY DAY ICING, &
earth orbits a dream. Poets do things, &
moons explode by cosmic impacts of
time. Nobody listens. A baby
cries a thousand poems from a dark
milk-odored crib. Little vampire crabs
scurry up the posts.

The Slaughter of Liberty

I can't say things without legal ramifications
ramming up my ass. I won't even retard details
to explain my situation of chained silence.
It is
also dangerous to pose questioning poems
anywhere on the internet, or aloud to consumers,
or to find the next word is a keyword monitored
by homeland security, so a pause, a deletion
occurs between brain & fingers.
I am a very gray man, mostly ghost. What
meat exists, what bones, blood, semen remain,
is me as a poet in Amerika. Censorship
has made me very ugly, leaves me grunting,
erases my positions. Bent on a cane, sound of
shuffling that used to be my screams.

Light Verse

Being a poet is a terrible thing
alone inside a small 2nd floor
room after midnight. He
is naked &
gross & drunk.

Grinding a flamboyant grouse
in a dream field with pressing elbows
for poetic luck, he spits at the sweet moon.
Poems blush. A professor stutters. He wears
bird bones in the sunny gin-soaked morning.

The world is a swallowed grouse.
He coughs up feathers, beaks, blood,
crushed claws & spiritual relief
to fly again, or to
feel he's flying.

Totally Fine

My daughter phones
after having a bad dream.
"Are you all right?" she
asks. I reassure
her I am totally fine,
totally fine, it was
just a dream. Her
voice sounds heavy
& weary, which feels
like the weight of
my soul.
Bare angst is
as sane as subatomic
evaporation where hours fog
mental terrain. *I am totally fine*, but
I do add like a wagging tail,
considering. I don't expound.
We talk about the kids.
She begins to sound better,
sighing & laughing,
pissed at the dog
who sheds & sheds & sheds.
Nobody's dreaming. I never
reveal to my psychic daughter
I am not totally fine.

Rainy Night Poem

I wish we remember to give my son
Bambi #2 for Trisha. Grandpa pre-ordered
it online. We keep forgetting. It's in the middle
room on Ann's desk with the receipt saying
We Love You Trisha, Grandpa & Ann. Maybe
this week, tomorrow? She'll
bubble excitement & *SMILE*. Walt Disney has
wormed into our very DNA, &

Bambi is such a sweet word. I knew a girl
named Bambi in high school. She had a
voice like a Disney character;
kind of dizzy, but man, her tits were amazing.
Full, spilling like pure honey-gold alchemy.
OK, I admit I pawed for them under a
train trestle in the woods, smoking, destroying
her trust forever. Stupid glandular kid.

It's a good miracle. Aging allows us to forgive
ourselves, to understand. The movie
Bambi #2
picks up in the middle of Bambi #1.
Everyone has seen the original
Bambi, or knows the story. Grandpa has
visions of Bambi probed by foggy
aliens, but that's just crazy Grandpa

wanting the world to rip open like caesarean
birth in the hands of Rob Zombie. Fuck yeah,

action blood & special effects. We are spiraling
edgeless waves of space/time fabric.
The vast seas rumble from squashing plum
electrons in Switzerland. Two molecular
deer leap, crash into each other, intermesh
for love, for Disney, for life at the end of

an epic. In the future Trisha
will not be surprised Bambi is used
as a logo to lure people with money
to the moon as a family vacation.
Powered by Disney & men
made of frogs, goat tongues & radiated
honey. Hologram flight attendants
are courteous & uniquely calming.

Bambi is a cereal, too. Bambi references
moon dust, a soft state of mind. Every
pacifier on the planet is a Bambi pacifier.
Bambi will end human feeling, all that
existential pain & worry. Bambi
will lick our troubles away. Jesus &
Bambi mate on the White House lawn,
elite, ecstatic, before aliens gang-rape

Earth's population of sweet deer &
our numbed heavenly soul holes.

When They Came over

Unwashed for months on a boat
to the shores of Amerikan freedom.
Possibilities of the imagination, seeds
for the future & prosperous lives; eventuality
knocks me like the brunt of a pistol
as I sit here by a great lake in
the 21st century staring at gray
paradox. You bastards didn't own

smart phones, drive 4-wheel-drive
computer cars, know hot-&-ready
pizza, flat screens, microwaves,
the microwavable. There were trees,
honeybees, rutted muddy roads
ending in deep black woods. Moon
over the world like an egg-colored
melon. You were lost so next

generations cld pursue & find happiness.
I hesitate to say gullible, naive, but the
land is cracking. Jesus plans on burning
down the sky on top of Chicago's
Sears Building. Point lightning bolts across
the curves of the world.
We're sunk here. We can't leave or enter
our borders without a passport &

genital x-ray. You raised cattle &
cowards. Roll in yr graves,

ring bone
bells.
I'm a flower
growing in yr dirt skull.
Modern methane
has turned my green leaves black.

Taking Tonight off Work

I intentionally
let the image of Delbert leaving
the shop burn in my mind. He's

retiring. Never again to see Delbert
except possibly in the obituaries.
I feel his final strong handshake.

My last image of Judy
this morning is
the side of her face in her

little red car pulling out of
the factory parking lot
forever. Then I think about

the rest of the shift.
A few of us with 20 years
to go before

retirement,
& all the fucking
ignorant Amerikan factory-rat kids:

those without history
& pain &
recurring echoes.

Cons,

union
liars. They stay.

It's like a
concentration camp
& the good, true,

honest,
ethical prisoners
are the first slaughtered.

Who remains, who endures
are those who say
yes yes yes

when a
gun barrel is
kissing their asshole.

What a disappointing
array of
hanger-on employees.

Nobody is left
to cheer.
Not Hillbilly,

that old
country-suspender fuck
with a big mouth

spitting
cursive snuff-juice

across the factory floor;

retired.
No more heroes
exist.

Just old losers
& young brash
shits.

Men
& women
have lived whole lives

in jobs
these motherfuckers
desecrate with idiocy.

An Oblong Balloon of Blood

When I was a stupid kid, before drugs,
booze, even before poetry,
I wore St. Christopher on a
chain around my neck. I went to
church &

catechism. I kissed a bishop's red ring
as he offered his hand to a row of us
after confirmation. Little tufts of wings
appeared because God pinched & pulled
tips of feathers thru our skin.

My brain was made of white milk,
Sky King, field grasshoppers, television
waves, pulverized June bugs, echoes
of world war victory, lawnmowers & bikes.
Sins were always erased by prayer.

It was a sunny autumn afternoon.
I joined a circle of Ellport guys
at the edge of the woods, wearing
my Little League baseball cap.
A burlap bag

hung from a low oak branch,
swaying from a rope. My friends
gripped baseball bats & thick
sticks, & everyone was smiling.
It was my turn to whack the cat.

143

The evil cat of an old witch.
Blood dripped from the
sack. I swung & hit it & another
cheer rose until that cat was
finally dead. I stopped

talking to God, & He stopped
caring about me after the cat
incident. I was wholly guilty.
My sins increased into major
sins, multiplying under

the rubbery sky. Brenda,
cum on her belly on a park
bench at dusk. Jay says
smoke it. Under age, beer &
pool tables, a purple Mustang.

College, acid sparks travel
decades ago.
Riding a bus, everyone
watches me giggle at their
cat eyes. I pretend I have insane claws.

Back in the States
I fall into a forklift job & stay
stoned. I love Sartre, quote
Nietzsche, blast loud Hendrix
over my hometown. Snort

cocaine Lisa gives me in a locked room.
This is before the abortion & my escape

to the west coast where I run a
lathe, high every day. I lick
an Eskimo chick.

I marry my pregnant girlfriend after
drinking 5 gin & tonics. The judge
doesn't finish his sentence, I'm laughing.
Maurice explains to Yr Honor he's just nervous,
he means no disrespect, then I'm legally married.

That marriage lasted 18 years. I knew hate.
A goat grew under my skin, I had horns.
The divorce was nauseating horror.
The burlap sack I'd beat as a kid
became that poor cat I helped murder as a man.

She

She wears a blue cotton blanket
like a flowing pyramidal gown
pretending she's Queen for a
Day, acting regal crossing
the cement cellar floor.
Seizing the blanket at her neck, she
balances a tiara crown made from an old
can. Her sister who still wets
the bed sits at a card table
applauding.
I realize I'm in love because I
want to marry the pretend queen.
I prize her & our new
washer. Blue eyes tear, & she
wins the world. I don't exist.

Closed Curtains

All winter I shut the 2 windows
with old curtains & dusty blinds.
Today is no different. There's
slush, air's above freezing.
I finally accept I am a
vulnerable man.
An atom of my mother's
breath laces the rest of the atoms
in my cracked cup.
Existence energy, sensory fuel.
Centuries of insemination.
Higgs
Blossom. I now feel
miraculous inside this dark
2nd story room.

Now that Morning Is Rising

Cats are fed, dishwasher empty, pot
of tea for transference
into two pitchers waits in the kitchen.

A bag of garbage to go outside into a blue
container in our garage – I figure I will
complete the tea & the garbage before I

procure a ladder to change the burned-
out backdoor light. There's a lot of snow &
ice, but the sky is halfway blue, & once

these chores are done
I can relax
either in a poem or aligned

on the couch with the television
playing something of interest on
Netflix.

Movies or shows Ann wld say
no to, but she's at work until
afternoon.

I'm hungry. Poetry,
every poem
ever composed is a lie & a

pain

in the active
ass.

Right Finger

This laptop is activated to my mind via finger-
print recognition below the keyboard. One
finger on my right hand crosses a white-blue
pulsating strip, & windows sing. Too fast,
white-blue turns agonizing orange – try again,
old fool. Yesterday I scrubbed the sink & things,
including, apparently, my fingerprint as far as
being known to my machine. Orange, orange,
slow as skin syrup, more honey than blood.
Orange, orange rod of computer light; as a backup,
of course, a specific password. The flowering
windows song. I look at my right forefinger thru
the bottom of my glasses, in desk lamplight,
& it is true, my swirling identification is sanded
smooth in tiny places, wine-streaks of red glass
rise. The top knuckle is blown inward like an
oak in continuous wind. Over 30 years in
factories demanding hands & muscles & silence
slaughtered these prehistoric formations, adding
arthritis, & poems.

With Breakfast

I am not going
outside into the
garage to see
if our old mower
starts, let a-
fucking-
lone
cut the grass
like most
neighbors,
since yesterday
was holy Easter
Bunny day.
An owl in a tree in
the park & daffodils
scream before
engines & voices, my
window wonderment,
wipe the backs of early beginnings.
Even Neanderthal ghosts are
as clean as glass-
clear humankind history.
Disappearance is crucial.
Discovery is crucial.
Scrubbing painful grass echoes
in half, part in hand crumbles
like burnt toast viced in a fist.
What is created & crushed
by lack is pancake

eternity with its beatnik snap
& sap, say *mmmm man maple*.

Tyger Eats Flowers

Tyger eats flowers, cellophane, Pop-
Tart packages, spiders, whatever
insects squeeze into our house. Card-
board edges, toast crumbs, tiny
pieces of pizza pepperoni. Ann walks
the dog & finds along our alley
a long, fresh red-yellow tulip
which she slides into a tall
green vase. Sets it on the
living room mantel. At night
the flower is placed in my
closed writing room. Tyger
eats flowers.
We always try for domestic
solutions in our
weird, problematic lives.

Monday Afternoon after

I'm sitting inside my stuffy room. No
list of shit is jotted. No descriptive
versification. No, I bitch-slap this poem
like backhanding a
gravestone since the ghost is oblivious.
Poetry isn't innocence.
Maybe the poet is. Maybe the walls are
turning, phones are singing, doors
open to close. Maybe
the poet is as guilty as all hell swinging
swords of bravado. Poetry is word blood.

Write from yr blood,
not yr brain or heart.
Gravity creates biped, ocean, stone, &
dream. Nouns sink thru ink plasma. Verbs
infect white cells.
There's a poet swaying on a
tightrope made from
the rocking breath of
sonnets.

Realigning Boris Pasternak

Reading Boris Pasternak this morning
I remember the fascinating feast
poetry served in my younger years.
Phrases fastened to astonishment urging me
to write. Quite a few poets pulled me into
the curious soup. Stone potatoes & wasp ash
pepper. Broth breath chicken & bread stew.
All mammalian limbs are really carrots
& green beans. I'm no fan of metered verse &
rhyme, but Boris Pasternak slapped my head
in the middle of one of his poems today. He
swings a gutted deer in the Russian woods,
orbital campfire smoke on his
Bolshevik hands.

To Have to Think

Age, as older people drop
off. The poets I knew are
dead & nobody remembers
their poems after initial
mourning. This angers me.
The poets spend their lives
writing, driving cabs, selling
turquoise, rolling in wheel-
chairs, running in some surf,
losing their money for poetry.
Losing their minds for poetry.
Dead poets drip like wax
over the eyes of ridiculous infants.
Decades pass without history.
Flash to the face of a pissed-
off, mascara-smeared, screaming
Courtney Love. The dead poets fail
to dent her soul.

Forcing the Force of a Smile

Ah, Karen Carpenter, you fill
the air of Amerika –
we hear you singing everywhere.
Latched to teenage feelings of
love, Karen, a perfect click. Topping
carnivals, fading from cars, background
speakers in family stores, across this great
land, pulsing by the light of the moon, baby,
we listen to yr songs & feel so goddamn
beautiful. But you were dying fast, we didn't
know, we cldn't even imagine. No, Karen
Carpenter had only just begun.
We're old people now who expect death,
irony galore, musical perversion. But yr
face as a young woman &
yr voice still make us
a little more beautiful than we ever were,
or are.

Afternoon Poem

This is a pipe.
This is tight green bud.

Dusty.
This is a black Bic lighter.

This is Ann imitating
W.C. Fields' "ah *yes.*" This

is me smiling.
"Do Mae West," I urge.

Soul Surgery with My Own Two Hands

Orange dust moths inside October pumpkins
eat black bat shadows. Meat of the fruit,
fruit of fire.

Good news is a 4-day weekend.
Relax, slow the spin & meditate.
It is soul repair

time. Dig into dark blood. Feel the
radiating pearl. This soul still has a pulse
& light. Circular memories.

Age is no illusion. Halloween
horror slashes flesh with axes of years.
Wounds, deformations. Poisonous

moon water. Stars melt chocolate.
A fingertip curls & spins
the pearl in blood.

Boiling a Bucket of Snow

Draped emissaries of the Pope gather
at our snowy back door. Wind cuts
the hedges at the side of the brick house.
It's afternoon, but the color of late evening.
All the way from Italy, the Vatican,
emissaries of the Pope knock on our
back door. We have yet to realize their
jet-lag drunkenness. Snow, the wind,
their red robes, hoods held tight around
their faces. I am able to make out
"His Holiness orders," from one of the
voices. I invite them inside. On her toes,
Ann is in another room hiding things.
They apologize for all the snow they're
tracking in, but I say, "Hey, we have a
dog. You guys
want some coffee or tea?" I ask to
shift the thought. Then they drop
their hoods: suns burn on their
shoulders. I figure I'm in some
deep shit. Ann is far
from being innocent, too.

Today

Branch screeches against bedroom
siding upstairs, wakes me as dark
wind accelerates, & I hear our back
door shut as Ann leaves for work.

5:30 alone in the house. Son
& granddaughter must be spending
the night with my ex-wife – hunting
season. I've never been a hunter. I

don't want to kill a deer, drag it thru
woods & gut it. No, it isn't
me. I can live without venison. I can
live because I haven't murdered another

mammal. Every mammal *feels*. My ex-wife
pleaded with me to hit her, screaming, on
fire in the kitchen of a lost house; I held
back, full of pulsation, & left to walk a

few blocks of the steam off. Yelling molecules
from my face, spitting hate, begging me to
slap the shit out of her, throw a fist.
I got out of there.

I didn't know then she had a boyfriend who
hunted. A large population of the citizenry of
Erie hunts; it's a popular sport, as I discovered
when I spent over 30 years in the factories. Ann's

opinion of hunting game is more pronounced an
attitude than mine, totally against even the
thought of killing an animal. She lets
spiders live. Ann blames "men" for our

nuclear arsenal, for wars & slaughter & politics.
We gift boys with BB guns & muscles, who naturally
grow into men with bigger weapons & more power.
She believes if women ruled, life

wld be less stressed, open, & flowering compassion.
I don't argue the founding fathers were clueless &
ignorant dismissing the genius of female brains.
Yes, the world has been mangled by the hands of

men from prehistoric times, & the brutal
chaos & corruptions & Congress, oh no
Congress, all the laws into the 1950s, male
testosterone from the balls of God, that

savage, bearded Being in the sky. Gently I attempt
to shift Ann's feminist stance & change
subjects. She knows I intentionally do this – she
knows me. Nobody else knows me. If I was alone

in the universe I wld kiss deer & flowers &
unadulterated air, & I wld have died a long
time
ago. Mutated by time, I am who I am. Ann

loves the internal me, my stardust. Because of
this inner soul trust, I love her stardust too. I

162

know I get out of hand at times, I'm totally human.
She scolds me so I understand, I get it, from

the voice of her heart. The level & balance.
Thank you, sweetheart, you're
my best blessing in this life.
It's afternoon. You'll be home. I'll be whole.

Wet Day

Ann is emptying the dishwasher
downstairs, glass tinkles, growling
drawers, pounding pans & shattering
doors, smack of dishes. She is wearing
yellow rubber gloves, the smallest size
they make. She's about a foot shorter
than me, almost half my weight.
This is when living
is more difficult by days rather than by
seasons or years, when less possibility
prisms the future. This is where trees
can't pull thru taffy streets any longer.
Where birds wreck & rock dissolves.
It's an old fucking sky, & an old world.
We know dishwashers, vacuums, knitting,
poems, television, movies, Monday night
is garbage night in this piece of the city.
The day is rotting snow, fog on the ground,
mist as sky. Memory rain this morning.
Who needs Buddha
inside a warm home.
Stop, have a seat.
I feel like melting, too.

The Door (uppercase lines to be read by Trisha, alternate lines by Grandpa)

THE DOOR IS OPEN. THE DOOR HAS EYES.

The door is closed. The door is a landslide of stone.

THE DOOR IS OPEN LIKE AN EXPLODED SKULL.

The door is closed against an orange ocean wave of ghosts.

THE DOOR IS OPEN LIKE A MOUTH SAYING BOO.

The door is a purple pearl rolling around in my head.

THE DOOR IS OPEN MIRRORS & MIRROR CREATURES.

The door is a wall & a floor & a ceiling, & another door.

THE DOOR IS A MOON CLOUD SMILING IN THE SKY.

The door is made of carrots, rusty rain & chicken language.

THE DOOR IS AN OPEN LEAF. THE DOOR IS A YELLOW
FLOWER.

The door is a closed clam. The door is made of black meat.

THE DOOR IS OPEN LIKE A JUMPING SKELETON WITH
BELLS.

It's almost Halloween. It's almost Halloween.

Before the Shit Hits the Fan

I always expected being the father
of 2 grown kids, with 5 grandchildren,

things wld get easier. The fight less
intense, no spiritual stakes. Just

getting old with a smile & poems
& grown kids & 5 grandchildren, old

eccentric Grandpa, Dad. That
was fairly stupid of me. I didn't

foresee the claws of chaos
chop peacefulness off the top

of my brain.
The snip, snip, snip.

Madly slapping pieces of my
brain back in, eventually

I give
up. Worms chill my feet. Living

long is always
vicious.

What Are You

What are you doing?

I'm rolling a fat marble
of night in my
hands. What are YOU doing?

Listening to edges of echoes
slit wrists & eardrums.
What are you doing now?

I allow my body to blossom
blindness &
precognition.

I pray
without teeth but with
poems. What are YOU doing now?

Fine nicotine laces my skin.
Pores bubble tarry amber.
My foggy hair levitates over

October. Over weird moons of the moon
the southern cosmos
defeats & slaughters all light.

What am I doing? Swimming
against a wave of skulls &
an endless skull horizon. Pork chops

hang & beard my chin. Prescription
glasses are made of round ham.
I am lighting a match

with my throat.

Who Gives a Shit

Nibbling on crunchy dead
cockroaches & hollow upturned
flies. Chewing a tree
for the faint sweetness of sap
turpentine. Gulp black rock soup
underneath wood mud.
Brain of a snake, a mushed pea
wiped onto the spoon of a finger,
edge to tongue, plus purple amoeba
sprinkles. The sky browns. Eggs are
almost full of rain. When cats are
food, the missiles whistle. Inside
dogs genetic bombs grow,
touch & explode. Pets gain
language & curse the world.

John Travolta

John Travolta is a snotty kid. The next baby generation behind us. Woodstock sculpts our minds, but Travolta has never heard of Woodstock. Woodstock starts to deteriorate when John infects all screens dancing like a loopy elastic robot, dressed like a phallic blue stud. He probably manicures his ballsack.

None of us can dance & not look like a fool. Nobody wears John Travolta's pants. We are the scraggly Ellport gang visiting a disco outside Pittsburgh. The floor is color-changing panels of pastel light, & the god-like disco ball spins strands of blood across the loud, ear-damaging room. We elbow our way to the bar, yelling over the music for our drinks. John Travolta is EVERYWHERE. But we're concentrating on females. Some of the girls swoon & touch John, kiss & twirl under spinning red drops; not them. It's the women who dance away from Travolta, backing up to dissolve in the coke-pulsing crowd we watch like smiling beady-eyed sharks. Cum oceans flap from our feverish gills.

King's Inn

I was a bartender at JJ's & also at King's Inn. The owners were friends, or the guy who ran JJ's, a disco strip club, owed a ton of money to the older guy who ran King's Inn. I did not know, but my services were required & traded. I went with it, I needed the money. That was the rationale, more money, & a promise there will be even more if I play it cool. The owner's name: George. His loud wife, Greta. George had a bodyguard, Frank, large as a walrus, about as intellectual as walrus snot. They all drank the expensive Walker, but Greta needed ice. George & Frank maintained on 4 straight fingers, neat. I always kept aware of the group at the bar. George smiled continuously when he spoke, "Don't charge that table over there. They're our friends, OK." I turned around inside my horseshoe station. 4 guys looked like the mob or something really fishy. I watched Cindy bend to ask what they wanted to drink. She was smiling. Not one of those creepy guys smiled. "On the house," Cindy sang as she set 4 bottles of beer & 4 clean glasses in the middle of their table. After pouring some into their glasses they cheered across the bar to George, & George raised his drink to the ceiling too as a disco light show rolled colors over everyone & everything, bright on the dancers, warm for the shadows lined by sex-hungry animals. I was in charge of the switches behind the bar for the lights & for the several tapes of disco I had to keep playing, but I cld adjust the volume & the speed of light circles. George acted reluctant to fire me, but he did. One of his rats, Rico, a big-time coke dealer, told George I had been in the kitchen snorting cocaine with him & some girls & had left the bar unattended after George & his crew left one night. I denied it, of course, yet George didn't believe me. He was smiling. I was, actually, lying. I hope Rico's dead. Rico also told George I was giving out free drinks. This was, again, true. Booze for coke & drugs. But such betrayal.

171

What You Are

Wrong, drunken madness, rude
views, I'm not denying anything.
I look at years of photographs
& feel sadness flood like bourbon.
Death fucks every granulated
atom rolling across earth.
We name time the 21st century.
We create test-tube monkeys from
God's last teardrop. I repeat my
father's jokes from the 1950s
which have lost all humor &
common sense & sensitivity.
Above his grave on a gray day
I sigh. Dad, the Mayans are
dancing like adverbial
adjectives.
Their bloody peepees
poke thru their green leaf
tutus.

Poisonous Echoes

You are dead because you will die.
Mental cancer decays the pulp
around yr soul like a peach pit
heaved & set wet in the center of
yr shoulders. Yr soul is in yr
skull, yr hollow, hollow skull.
You roll in peach pulp to achieve
the darkest enlightenment.
Postponement. Dancing
in cow shit is a little zest but not
necessary. The soul pit,
talking peach, split by a
time hammer, is full of dust.
Not even dust. Infectious silence.

Tip

I am always writing my first
poem & I am always writing
my last poem & I am always
writing between poems. Stop
motion, I'm mute. The day
easy, hey, stay away. I am
always writing a mushed, crushed
poem & I am always writing a
poem made from chipped rock
& I am always writing a poem
mothered from the V of the alphabet.
Fluctuation is very ticklish. Silence
hears, which is why we never hear
silence. I like talking with my mouth
shut, using my tongue for mind
words. Maybe it's the dopamine
level at birth, genetic adjustments.
Something savagely biological. Behind
false teeth a crushed worm clicks &
wiggles & the feeling nears sexual
texture. A natural, oral delicacy.
Her deep oysters. I am always
writing a poem using scissors &
black paper sheets. I'm 13 years old
with cum webs between my fingers;
I'm always thinking about death
being 61. I am always writing a
poem scripted by a gold feather;
quill-tip, the tiny skull of a blood
drop.

Notes for TV Interview

I was living in College Park, Maryland, with a friend from Point Park College. She was doing graduate work at the University of Maryland, but living by herself in married-student housing since the rooms were larger. Somehow she manipulated this, & when I phoned her with my many troubles at the time – around 1977 – girlfriends I needed to escape from, no money, no job, she invited me down to live with her. I packed my old flip-switch ignition clunker with clothes & books & poems, & drove south. We had a fine arrangement; she had classes during the day, & I either worked temporary jobs or stayed in the living room hand-writing poems. The college was a mile walk, & I found a shortcut where I happened to pass an interesting-looking bookstore. I found Gargoyle, Issue 4 I think, & bought the magazine. I felt immediate kinship with the editor, Rick Peabody, tho our letters crossed in the mail after I submitted some typed poems, but then had to leave College Park & Sandy to return home.

Back in my hometown of Ellport, I quickly found work at the sewage treatment plant. My boss was Greg, a year older than me, a recent Penn State graduate, living with his parents. I spent a lot of my time writing & reading there, & after work Greg & I wld meet our gang at the Oak Grove Inn or the other Ellport bar, but because our friend Regis had been banned from entering that bar, we mostly met up at Oak Grove to gulp pitchers of beer & shoot pool.

I had never stopped writing poetry, even so young & hungover. I continued the paper relationship with Rick Peabody, who suggested other magazines I shld submit to, & I did, & basked in the glory of artistic recognition.

This was all happening via the United States Postal Service, submissions, magazines, books, letters, postcards, mail-art, cassettes from England, from West Germany, & all happening simultaneously to bartending at 2 bars, crazy dive women, then I was married & we had an infant daughter.

We were living in Auburn, state of Washington, where I found work at a ladder factory making the rungs. The mail connections increased.

When I moved to Erie in 1980, it was because we didn't feel right denying our parents their grandchild, & because my sister was married & living in Erie after graduating from Gannon University, & my brother-in-law thought he cld get me a job in the plastic injection molding factory where he was a boss. We flew east on a credit card I knew I'd never pay. We paid a moving company to pack our belongings, & next I'm living on 26th Street in a lower duplex with a wife & baby & accumulations. It took me 3 months to start that factory job. We were living on pennies. I walked a good 2 miles to the steady 2nd-shift job in the middle of winter. The front room became my writing room. My typewriter, books, papers, letters, a thrilling mailbox – a letter from Bukowski, wild art-written cards from S. Clay Wilson of *Zap* fame, signed copies of chapbooks from poets I liked – big names & the unknowns (then).

I decided to produce my own small-press lit mag, Northern Pleasure, soon after reading an essay in the Erie Sunday Times from an established poet in the city. This guy was quoting Longfellow, & sounded like he was totally out of touch with the reality I knew was happening in the underground scene at the time. I wrote a letter to him, admonishing him for portraying poetry in such a bullshit way. Poetry was alive, poetry was vital, poetry was occurring & full of roaring energy. He wrote me a terse note back, but then in the surprising mailbox I got a letter from John Vanco of the Erie Art Museum inviting me to read at a place called Clayspace under the bridge at State & 15th.

The reading was great. John had made sure there was a good supply of Rolling Rock beer. I met Lonnie Sherman there, & Lenny Bove who came up to me with a bottle of blackberry brandy, all excited, yelling RON RON I DIDN'T KNOW THIS KIND OF STUFF WAS HAP-PENING IN ERIE! I read some pretty rebellious poems as I recall, drunk off the beer.

John Vanco was close friends with Lonnie Sherman, a pure poet heavily influenced by the Beats. Lonnie & I became friends. He is the only poet I know who has brought tears to my eyes listening to him read. We traveled together to various readings – Buffalo, Pittsburgh, Kent. Lonnie & his friend Rick Lopez began publishing Kangaroo Court. Lonnie & Lopez brought Jack Micheline to Erie to read, thanks to a grant via the Erie Art Museum. A true Beat, Micheline was living off any readings he cld muster. Lonnie & Lopez also brought Todd Moore to Erie. Todd & I were friends from the early days; his letters to me were these big ink scrawls over pages & pages. There were a bunch of other readings, some in Erie, that I participated in.

After 4 issues of Northern Pleasure, I felt burnt out & not up to all the xeroxing, collating, stapling, & mailing, but that didn't stop the mail-box from bringing gifts from heaven.

I have a very difficult time when listing credits for a bio because my poems were being published all over the place. I'd send in a stack of poems to a press & next I'd see them published as a chapbook.

In 1984 Zen Sutherland, who then lived in Virginia, drove up in a junker & we traveled west together. Zen was publisher of Mockersatz Press at the time – wild, weird stuff – an absolute madman & genius.

We drove to Detroit to meet Kurt Nimmo who lived down a dark & dangerous street. Kurt published Planet Detroit then. We all got very hammered & stumbled to the train tracks to scream spontaneous poems at the night sky. What I think connected us, related us, was our poetic insistence for reality, vis-a-vis "the real shit" of existence, as poets in the 1980s.

Kurt had a gun in his boot. He wasn't writing about academic indulgences. Nimmo was kicked to the streets of Detroit right after graduating high school. He was not only a savage poet, but had the fury of other art, collage, music, painting, thinking from a place no man has thought – a rare, original voice at the edge of Detroit. We'd all known about each other thru the mail, had work in the same magazines, etc. Meeting Kurt for the first time, he's all old black leather while Zen & I are lunatic clowns, yet we coalesce.

Then Zen & I drove to Chicago to the beautiful brick house of Steve Doering, editor of Random Weirdness, & Steve's mother. She nursed us back to health after Detroit (Nimmo's bathroom didn't work, there was an amp & some wires in the dry bathtub). We got showers & food.

Todd Moore arrived at Steve's the next afternoon. He didn't live far away. He talked about poetry as an action. Political, societal, cultural mirroring. Poetry was such an important involvement. Did Zen & I visit any other poets? Maybe. The car broke down in Painesville, Ohio, so I had to call my then-wife to come in our car & pick us up.

The next day, Zen insisted he was hitching his way back home. Both of us knew whatever happened wld be poetry. The next time I saw him, Lonnie & I had traveled down to Pittsburgh to a reading, then a party at Harry Calhoun's apartment on a hill overlooking the city. Rick Peabody had driven up from D.C. with editors John Elsberg & David Greisman. Michael Basinski, archivist at SUNY Buffalo, gave me a ride back to Erie, tho I sneezed most of the way: Zen had procured a tank of nitrous oxide, & a big bag of balloons. It's where I first met Cheryl Townsend & also Don Wentworth. It was a wild party/reading. It went out live over Pittsburgh airwaves via some college, tho I imagine somebody had sense enough to push the off button after an older, mature woman read poems about death as we in the crowd filled & sucked balloons, breaking into laughs.

It was a reading at Hemingway's in Pittsburgh where Bart Solarczyk introduced himself, bearded & big like Bluto. Bart & I took many road trips together in the name of poetry. I cld never drink as much beer as Bart. He was publisher of Burnt Orphan Press. He came up to Erie for some reading series via the Erie Art Museum, when Paul Weinman stepped on stage in the nude to read his White Boy rants.

Paul had recently been on the cover of the Albany newspaper burning an Amerikan flag on the steps of the Capitol. Around the edges of the photograph, veterans in hats screaming & pointing at his face, at his very point. Paul & I co-produced around 20 pamphlets together. We called them "spoofs." One was titled "More Odd," spoofing Todd Moore. We did Plath, Swinburne, Kerouac, The Three Stooges, a wide range of subjects. All is supposedly in vaults at SUNY Buffalo.

As my marriage was ending, I bought a box called WEBTV, & found the instant internet on television in my living room. Nimmo was active. Jim Chandler. Lots of other writers I knew by way of paper were now electronic.

Michael McNeilley, who was living in Port Townsend, Washington, helped me stay together during that tough time via the internet & immediacy. His press was The Olympia Review, & McNeilley was a master poet whose work I greatly admired. He designed an online message-board for me, Pressure Press, & the response was delight, poets

179

suddenly splashing the screen of the television in my face; late 90s, early 2000s, the internet was a Wild-West party. This occurred simultaneously to hooking back up with Ann, my true love. I met her at Franconia College in New Hampshire, then out of the blue she phones me some 20 years later just as I was in the
process of divorce, & so was she. Pressure Press had much to do with Ann, also. It was an active board, with conversations, with poems, with seductions, with drunk-ass anger, from people all over the country & the world.

Way too soon, McNeilley passed away. His early web-designing was brilliant & interactive. Then a regular to the message board, Bill Beaver, offered to resurrect the site as close to the original as he cld, the blue background, buttons of offerings like photographs. We remained Pressure Press, tho I may have added "precognitive" or "prelapsarian" to the title.

Magic happened all the time: a poem from a poet in New Jersey, for instance, posted at 3:00 in the morning full of lust, or, after seeing the sun shade green, somebody includes such an image in a poem – a primal, mythological piece of star dust flowing thru world-wide cables a few mere seconds behind the speed of light. We even arranged parties on the board, announcing this is when we will be online & we will be drinking & please come to our party in cyberspace & hell yes those were good times.

It was up for a few years, & then I started Pressure Press on the Ning network. Soon it transmigrated onto Facebook as a closed group site, where there are a bunch of cool features & years of archives. Pressure Press does have much of the original wild blood, like it did when the internet was a new form, not a basic form, of communication. I post some of my poems there. It's an isolated but active place on the net. Poets shld maintain a lonesomeness, an outsider perspective.

Poetry isn't mindless mud entertainment, tho it can be. Words are made of breath & blood. This premise goes back to William Carlos Williams & the essays of Charles Olson, back to Robert Creeley, back to Pound, the insistence that a poem be organic. "No ideas but in things," Williams said. He described poetry as a bag of words, tho this may be because he was a full-time family doctor in New Jersey who carried a doctor's bag.

In my correspondence with the poet Larry Eigner, disabled by multiple sclerosis, he took issue with a bag of words & widened my eyes with his dictate that a poem is a BIOLOGICAL construct, a BODY of words. I take that to heart. A poem has to breathe by way of rhythm & sound – sometimes poems have to use the square of a page & create the silence between music, which is also music. My poems are page-oriented, & words made of blood & breath are knitted by my self with the tools I know that create poetry from the life I live.

I remember reading an early interview with Creeley in which he flat-out warns that "a poet lives by his or her wits." It isn't required that a poet be a college professor; a poet can be an auto mechanic, a plumber, a factory worker. A poet must write whatever the fates slap into being. This was an awareness I developed early in my 20s, the importance of poetry no matter what the poet lives. I am thankful for my college exposure & immersion into the history of modern Amerikan poetry, but it's what happened AFTER college that transmigrated into poetry for me. I loved reading Frank O'Hara, for instance, when he's eating a tuna sandwich in NYC & it's all first-person intense writing. His poems feel like they dance. The dimensional aspect is relevant, using all the senses of a human, including the 3rd eye, in a poem. Todd Moore taught me that poems can be vivid, visual scenes, but also smell of nicotine & bourbon & gun powder.

I don't think it's been realized yet, this history, as we roll into the 21st century like a poetry snowball rolls down an endless-looking hill, but right now, evolutionary miracles happen. A poem shld be read for its surprise, its new sense. "Make it new," Ezra Pound says, his impenetrable work be damned. A natural cadence of structure per Olson's dictum of place & history: we must know the past to produce the future. I only mean this as poetry, not culture, which is so out-of-hand it's blatantly ridiculous & all about money. Poetry is so worthless, it's one of a few treasures remaining in the country.

My poetry professor at Franconia College was Robert Grenier (then aged 27!) who had studied with Robert Lowell at Harvard, who had personally partied with Charles Olson, who brought in some Black Mountain poets like Alice Notley, Clark Coolidge, Eigner & Creeley, to read & interact with the students. This was a rare opportunity, & something I cherish. Joel Oppenheimer made fun of a word I used in a poem I recited in Grenier's class there; the word was "polish" as in shine, but this purple-hatted poet didn't see it like that. I was devastated by his cruel critique. My poetry had to be deconstructed, & it was, with their suggestions, unintentional & intentional. I had to bleed to know blood. I had to obliterate before I cld create. I'd been writing "love poems," poems with a kid's emotion. Letters from Eigner ground that to pieces. Look at poetry from a cerebral aspect, as internal speech or expression caught by the throat & given breath, to breathe, to mirror invisibility. Olson's Projective Verse helped to open my voice – adjustments of frequency, until tuned like a living instrument. Language is the medium.

I've done several collaborations with musicians & also painters/artists. One day in the mail I got a magazine from France, mostly by photographers, but sprinkled in the slick pages were world-wide poets, & there was a poem I wrote. Odd magic such as that does occur. Years ago, at some time in the 90s, I got a letter out of the blue from Vincent Ferrini

182

– I knew of his name, his association with Olson, but he wrote simply to say he appreciates my writing.

My recent collaborations with artists, via Didi Menendez & her absolute professionalism in cyberzines as art on their own, have been energizing. Much of my recent work can be found in the interrelated projects of Didi Menendez. If there's an audience interested in my poetry, great; if not, no sweat. I'm a poet. I've been living in Erie since 1980. Whether anyone cares, I've written decades into poems. Some people play piano, I play poems.

A poem must invade the brain of the eventual invader, poem & reader switch reactions & neuronal alleyways. I like poems like Raymond Carver's; the words are naturally nude, but bulge with paradoxical insight & inspirational light.

BIOGRAPHY

Ron Androla is a poet who lives in Erie, Pennsylvania with his wife, Ann. His work has been published extensively in print & online since the 1970s. Some of his books (some available via *Amazon*) include:

The Water of Mars (Createspace, 2013); *Maybe There Are Mathematics* (Createspace, 2013); *Quantum Aquarium* (MiPOesias, 2012); *What To Say To Death* (GOSS183::CASA MENENDEZ, 2008); *Poet Head*, selected poems 2001-2005 (Rank Stranger Press, 2005); *POT POET* (Rank Stranger Press, 2005); *You Know How It Goes* (Fingerprint Press, 2004); *It's a Pretty World* (Non Compos Mentis Press, 1996); *Splattered in Erie* (Smiling Dog Press, 1996)

Journals & e-zine credits include:

Atom Mind, Chiron Review, Gargoyle Magazine, Poetry Motel, Poets & Artists, IARTISTAS, OCHO, Red Fez, Wooden Head Review, Thunder Sandwich, Busted Dharma, Zygote in My Coffee, & many more.

Ron was awarded the Erie Poet Lifetime Achievement Award in 2013.

www.ingramcontent.com/pod-product-compliance
Lightning Source LLC
LaVergne TN
LVHW051308080426
835509LV00020B/3159